Progressive Gaelic 1

Moray Watson

Copyright © 2011 Moray Watson

Second Edition 2012

Follais Books, Aberdeen

All rights reserved.

ISBN: 1478233257
ISBN-13: 978-1478233251

DEDICATION

This book is dedicated to all my Gaelic students, past and present, who teach me so much about the language. The book is also dedicated, with much thanks and respect, to Dr Seumas Grannd, from whom I acquired my knowledge of the language in the first place. I have no doubt that his excellent teaching style has influenced the content, and I can only hope that the book in some way does justice to him. Any errors or infelicities are, however, entirely my own work.

CONTENTS

	Introduction	i
1	Introducing the Verb 'to be'	1
2	The Other Verb 'to be'	10
3	Answering 'yes' and 'no'	20
4	Introducing Nouns and 'the'	29
5	The Spelling Rule and The Present Tense	38
6	Masculine Nominative Singular	46
7	Feminine Nominative Singular	54
8	The Past Tense of the Verb 'to be'	63
9	Plurals, Possession and Imperatives	71
10	Masculine Dative Singular	82
11	Feminine Dative Singular	90
12	The Past Tense	99
13	Emphatic Pronouns and Prepositional Pronouns	112
14	Future Tense of the Verb 'to be'	120
15	Negative Questions	130
16	More Notes on Verbs	137
17	The Future Tense	148
18	Expressing Possession and Ownership	158
19	Using the Copula for Emphasis	165
20	Expressing the Infinitive	172
21	Irregular Verbs and Possessive Pronouns	180
22	Pronouns as Direct Objects, and Past Participles	190
	Appendix: Prepositional Pronouns	197

INTRODUCTION

Learning Gaelic

Learning a language is a big commitment, but is one of the most rewarding experiences you will undertake in your life. When you reach the stage where you can consider yourself to be 'fluent', you will give yourself a huge metaphorical pat on the back, and you will be highly deserving of that. A language is more than just a collection of words, sounds and structures: it is a doorway into another culture, a way of adding to how you see the world. If all cultures perceive the world at least slightly differently, your perception is enhanced and enriched every time you add another language to your repertoire. If Gaelic is the first language you have learnt since you acquired your mother tongue, I hope the experience will inspire you to go on and study more languages. If it does, you will also be delighted to discover that the experience of learning one additional language actually makes it easier to learn another (and another and so on).

Celtic

Gaelic is a Celtic language, and, more specifically, a Q-Celtic language. This means it belongs to the Indo-European group. It is therefore distantly related to English, German, French, Spanish, Dutch, etc., but the relationship is very hard for most of us to see. It is more closely related to the other Celtic languages, such as Welsh, but even here the relationship is not obvious. It is much more closely related to Irish and Manx. With a good knowledge of Gaelic, some basic tips about Irish or Manx, and the aid of a dictionary, it is possible to read certain texts in one of the other languages or even to take part in a stilted conversation. Many of the features of Gaelic that linguists find peculiar are also true of the other Celtic languages (e.g. the lack of 'yes' and 'no' or the verb 'to have'). This is why Gaelic is studied in Celtic departments in universities, and you may well find that you will want to know more about Celtic languages once you have acquired a good grasp of Gaelic.

Where Gaelic is Spoken

Gaelic was once the main language of most of Scotland (including the North-East), but it has gradually receded to the north and west, since about the twelfth century. The last speakers of Aberdeenshire Gaelic probably died out over a century ago, and most speakers now come from the Western Isles, the west coast, the Argyll islands, or Skye. Because of the economic situation in many of these places, emigration has been commonplace for many years, and so around half of all Gaelic-speakers now live in areas where Gaelic is not an 'everyday language' – e.g. Glasgow, Edinburgh, Aberdeen, Stirling, etc. Emigration is nothing new to the Gaelic world: since the late eighteenth century, very large numbers of Gaels have moved to other parts of the British Isles and all over the world. The numbers of emigrants were so large that Gaelic communities were established in other countries. The largest and most well-known of these was in Canada. There is still a notable Gaelic presence in Canada, most especially in Nova Scotia, where there is still a small community of native speakers and a larger group of people who are learning the language.

Gaelic Today and Job Opportunities

Gaelic has been enjoying a tremendous revival in fortunes in the past few years. In particular, there is a new understanding among the general population of Scotland that the language is one of our national treasures, which, along with Doric, Orcadian, Shetlandic, other varieties of Scots, and the music and storytelling traditions of the various parts of the country, should be held in high esteem and preserved for future generations. With this understanding, there is a new political will to try to reverse some of the damage that the centuries of anti-diversity policies had done to the language. As a result, there are now more and more job opportunities opening up for people who know the language. Gaelic graduates are in great demand, and that demand seems destined to keep increasing over the coming years.

Using this Course, and How to Learn

This is not a self-teaching course. You will get the most out of the textbook if you use it as part of a structured course with a teacher. The course is specifically designed for the Aberdeen University *ab initio* Gaelic stream, and it assumes that you will have at least four contact hours with Gaelic teachers each week. There are exercises in the textbook, but you will also benefit from using a workbook to ensure that you have understood each point before moving on. Learning a language is a highly progressive activity: each new stage depends heavily on your having mastered the one before. So, if you are experiencing difficulty at any time, you should address that problem immediately, rather than ignoring it and hoping all will become clear later. On the other hand, your teacher will sometimes suggest that you should leave some questions until later: this is educated advice, based on the knowledge that some answers given too early in the learning process actually lead to greater confusion. Please be guided by the teachers' experience when they give you answers like these: although it is frustrating to be told to wait, it is better than being given an answer that leaves you with ten times more questions!

Each unit in the course is built around two things: vocabulary and the structure of the language. The teacher will help you learn the structures, but *you* must learn the vocabulary. There is simply no way to learn a language without committing thousands of words to memory. Since most of us can only learn a few at a time, the course encourages you to do exactly that: every day, you will encounter a small number of new vocabulary items (your 'daily dose'). If you make sure you learn these as you go along, the effort you will need to make will seem small. If you refuse to learn the words as you go along, you will soon struggle to keep up in class, and you will either have several hundred words to learn during revision week, or you will set yourself up to fail the exam. This is such an important point that I am going to say it again: you **must** learn the vocabulary, and you must keep learning it several days a week, every week of the course (not just on days when you have classes).

Because vocabulary learning is so important, you should get hold of a small notebook that you can use to record your words. This should be a separate book from the one you use to record notes about the structure of the language etc. Make sure you get a vocabulary notebook that is small enough to fit easily into a pocket. I tend to prefer soft-cover notebooks and I avoid spiral-bound ones, as they are uncomfortable to carry in pockets. Take your vocabulary notebook to every class. Write down any new words (even if they are in your books) and any extra information you get (e.g. the gender of a noun, the plural form, the root of a verb, an idiom related to the word, etc.). Add in your daily vocabulary dose as well, and make it a priority to learn these words first before you try to learn your 'extra' vocabulary. Keep your notebook with you every day. If you are standing for ten minutes at a bus stop, take your book out and learn a word. If you are waiting for the kettle to boil to make your evening cuppa, take your book out and learn a word. If you are early for a class, take your book out and learn a word. If you are taking a break from a textbook you are reading for another course, or from typing an essay, take your book out and learn a word... With this approach, learning vocabulary becomes part of your daily routine and stops being a chore. As an added bonus, you have a new way of staving off the boredom of some of the little hiatuses in life!

Some people find it helpful to learn words by different kinds of association. For instance, some people have very visual memories. For these people, pictures can help them with vocabulary learning. You can use the internet to find pictures to attach to your vocabulary, for example. It is possible to buy sticky labels fairly cheaply. Some people find it useful to write down their vocabulary on labels and stick them to items all over the flat/house, so that they will see the Gaelic word whenever they look at the item. Other people find mind-mapping extremely helpful. By grouping words together into mind maps and other diagrams, some people find that it is easier to learn larger numbers of words. Similarly, if you are learning words that 'feel' closely-related (e.g. adjectives and their opposites – learn 'big' and 'small' together etc.), then try to group them when you learn them. For some people, it is helpful to learn words like 'open' and 'shut' at the same time, or 'walk' and 'run', etc. The course tries to group vocabulary like this, to some extent, but we also recognise that these kinds of associations are often peculiar to the individual, so it is up to you to organise your vocabulary-learning.

This course book does not cover the pronunciation of the language. The Aberdeen University Gaelic courses include other modules which deal with pronunciation issues. Similarly, this course does not give cultural information, beyond the basic concepts you might need in order to understand an idiom. Again, other modules within the programme deal with these issues. Good books are now available on both the pronunciation of the language and the cultural aspects of Gaelic, and you are encouraged to do some research to track these down.

'Other Information'

Most units have a few boxes marked 'Other Information'. These are little snippets of information that have been provided for the sake of people who are plagued by questions. If you are not feeling curious, or if you are finding it hard enough to understand the key information in that unit, feel free to ignore the 'Other Information' for now.

'Technical Terms Used in this Unit'

You do not have to be an expert on grammatical terms to learn a language. However, the more you know about these terms, the easier it is to grasp the explanations when you are being taught. This also helps to make it easier to learn other languages later on. Furthermore, although this book is written as a language course, it is also supporting a component of a university degree, and you should expect there to be some content which is more academic in nature than what might be found in a more informal course. The course is designed to give you the opportunity to move towards fluency in Gaelic, but it is also designed to enhance your metalinguistic awareness and to introduce you to the academic study of language. True, full fluency comes after several years of both study and practice: you will have to invest many hours into both the academic learning and the practice.

The course assumes only a very basic prior knowledge of grammatical terms. Each unit begins with a short explanation of the new terms that you will encounter in the unit. Some students may, in fact, be very familiar with these terms already. If this is true of you, then you will experience no difficulty if you ignore the 'Technical Terms Used in this Unit' section. The terms that are glossed in the unit also appear in bold throughout that unit, so that students are reminded that they can look them up. In the event that you read the explanation of a term in the book and you find that you still do not understand it, you should feel free to ask the teacher for help. The same technical terms are listed in alphabetical order at the back of the course book, in case you forget where they first came up. Just in case this is not enough help, some of the more central terms are also explained within the body of the text, in their own little boxes.

You will probably find the Technical terms glossary at the start of each chapter most useful if you use it for reference: i.e. instead of trying to read through it and remember it all, just look it up when you come across a word you are unsure of when reading the text.

Outline of the Language

Many people find it easier to learn something when they have a sense of what they have to expect. For this reason, I have made a list of some of the most important features of the Gaelic language. There is absolutely no need to learn this list, or even to understand it. In fact, you can ignore it completely if you think it is unlikely to help you.

Among other things, Gaelic has the following features:

- Only three main tenses: past, future and 'conditional';
- Therefore, no present tense: everything in the present is usually expressed by the verb 'to be' (which alone does have a present tense);
- Two verbs that express 'to be': one is used for the purposes of defining or emphasising, while the other is used for descriptive purposes;
- Four cases: 'nominative', dative, genitive and vocative;
- No verb 'to have': so possession is expressed using *aig* or *le*;
- No straightforward words for 'yes' and 'no': agreement or disagreement are expressed using the verb that was in the question;
- A system of prepositions and pronouns joining together (equivalent to this would be English forming words like 'atme', 'atyou' out of 'at' & 'me', 'at' & 'you' etc.);
- Two genders (or categories) of nouns, known as masculine and feminine;
- Only about eleven irregular verbs;
- Only a small group of defective verbs (i.e. verbs that have bits of tenses 'missing');
- Three main word orders for most verbs (verb-subject-object; auxiliary-subject-verb; auxiliary-subject-direct-object-verb);
- A system of suffixes that make certain words emphatic (equivalent to putting stress on words in English);
- No indefinite article (word for 'a' or 'an');
- Various definite articles (words for 'the'), which are mostly rather similar;
- Various ways of making nouns plural;
- A fairly large vocabulary, which is working hard to keep up with advances in modern technology, with the result that many contemporary words are familiar to English speakers(e.g. 'telebhisean' for 'television');
- A highly expressive idiomatic everyday language;
- A written language that goes back to ancient times and has a very logical spelling system, which nevertheless sometimes causes English speakers some difficulties and which is still not quite settled;
- Two main counting systems: one decimal (based on tens) and one vingesimal (based on twenties);
- Separate number words for counting people.

UNIT 1: 'TO BE' (1)

Technical Terms Used in this Unit

noun
: A 'naming' word. All <u>things</u> that can be listed are nouns: *table, cat, pen, milk, cloud, grass*, etc. If they are things that you can see, touch, etc., we say that they are **concrete nouns**. Things that cannot be seen or touched etc. are **abstract nouns**: *love, fun, indication, understanding*, etc. Names of people and places are sometimes called **proper nouns**. In Gaelic (as in English), proper nouns usually have capital letters when written down.

verb
: A 'doing' or 'being' word. A verb is a word that tells you about an action or state. The word underlined in each of these examples is a verb: 'I <u>ran</u>', 'John <u>spoke</u> to his friends', 'she <u>was</u> happy'. In the last example here, we have the verb 'to be', which is an important verb in English and Gaelic (in English, *am, are, is, was, were*, etc.). Gaelic has two verbs that mean 'to be'.

copula
: The copula is one of the two verbs 'to be'. It has the special function of joining two nouns or a noun and a pronoun: e.g. 'The <u>car</u> is a <u>Mazda</u>'; '<u>He</u> is a <u>teacher</u>'.

pronoun
: A pronoun is a word that can stand in for a noun (e.g. to avoid boring repetition). Examples in English include 'I', 'you', 'we' and 'they'.

definite noun
: When we talk about '<u>the</u> teacher', '<u>the</u> book', '<u>the</u> character', we are not just talking about any teacher, book or character: we have a specific one in mind. The word 'the' tells us that we are talking about that particular one. We say that 'the' makes the noun **definite** (it 'defines' which one we mean out of all the possible teachers, books, characters, etc. we could have been talking about).

definite article
: A word that is used to make a noun definite is called a **definite article**. In English, there is only one definite article: 'the'. Gaelic has several.

indefinite noun
: When a noun is not **definite** (see above), it is **indefinite**, and therefore we could be talking about any instance of that thing. In English, 'book' is an indefinite noun, as the word could refer to any book. '<u>A</u> book' is also indefinite.

indefinite article
: A word that can be put beside a noun to indicate that it is an indefinite noun is called an **indefinite article**. In English, the indefinite articles are 'a' and 'an'. Gaelic has none.

Faclan an Latha ... Your Daily Dose of Vocabulary

Key Words and Phrases

is mise...	*I am...*	**seo**	*this/here*
is esan...	*he is...*	**sin**	*that/there (fairly near the speaker)*
is ise...	*she is...*	**siud**	*that/there (farther away from the speaker)*

Nouns

càr (m)	*car / a car*	**an càr**	*the car*
leabhar (m)	*book / a book*	**an leabhar**	*the book*
taigh (m)	*house / a house*	**an taigh**	*the house*
peann (m)	*pen / a pen*	**am peann**	*the pen*
bòrd (m)	*table / a table*	**am bòrd**	*the table*
cathair (f)	*chair / a chair*	**a' chathair**	*the chair*

Verbs

thuirt	*said*
is	*am, is, are*

'To be'

Is mise...	I am...	Seo	This/here
Is esan...	He is...	Sin	That/there (fairly near the speaker)
Is ise...	She is...	Siud	That/there (farther away from the speaker)

You use *is mise* to introduce yourself. Examples:

Is mise Ruaraidh.
Is mise Calum MacLeòid.
Is mise Seònaid Nic a' Phearsain.

> What do you think the English versions of these three people's names might be?

The phrase contains the **verb** *is*, which is the **verb** 'to be' in Gaelic. Although it looks like a part of the English **verb** 'to be', the pronunciation is different. The Gaelic **verb** *is* is known as the **copula**. The **copula** is used for certain, specific roles. The two main jobs of the copula are: (1) it joins two **nouns**, or a **noun** and a **pronoun**; and (2) it emphasises a part of the sentence. In the phrase *is mise*, the copula is joining the **pronoun** *mise* with the person's name, which is a **noun**.

> **Other information:**
>
> Note, the phrase *is mise* is often pronounced, and sometimes written, as *'s mise*, and the two words sound like they run together.

There are various ways of introducing someone else into the conversation. You could use *is esan* ('he is') or *is ise* ('she is'), followed by the name. Or you could simply say *seo*, followed by the name.

> **Other information:**
>
> If you introduce someone by saying *seo*, the **copula** is implied. You are really shortening the phrase *is e seo* ('this is').

Exercise 1A:

1. Introduce yourself to the person next to you;
2. Introduce the person next to you to someone else.

Remember that the **copula** is used to join two **nouns** and to emphasise a part of the sentence. You CANNOT use the **copula** to make statements like 'I am tired', 'I am working', 'I am ugly'. These kinds of statements require the other Gaelic **verb** 'to be'.

> **Other information:**
>
> Use *seo*, *sin*, and *siud* with caution for the moment. There is another rule that you need to learn about how to use them in other contexts.

Using the copula to make sentences

Apart from using it to introduce yourself, you also use the **copula** to make sentences that require two **nouns/pronouns** to be linked. Normally, if the **copula** is used with an **indefinite noun**, the sentence requires a special tag line.

Examples:

'S e càr a th' ann.
It is a car.

'S e leabhar a th' ann.
It is a book.

'S e taigh a th' ann.
It is a house.

Notice the tag line *a th' ann*, which is a shortened version of *a tha ann*. This is the part of the sentence which tells you that the **noun** is **indefinite**. We will deal with **definite nouns** later.

Exercise 1B. Translate to Gaelic:

1. It is a pen.
2. It is a table.
3. It is a chair.

To make the sentence negative, you need the negative particle *cha*. This word is used with all **verbs** to show that they are negative.

Examples:

Chan e càr a th' ann.
It is not a car.

Chan e leabhar a th' ann.
It is not a book.

Chan e taigh a th' ann.
It is not a house.

Notice that when *cha* appears before a vowel (even when the vowel is in the next word), it changes to *chan*.

Other information:

If you are very observant, you will have noticed that the verb itself has disappeared in the negative. This is very unusual, and only happens with the copula. With all other verbs, the negative word *cha(n)* will appear along with a part of the verb itself.

Exercise 1C. Translate to Gaelic:

1. It is not a pen.
2. It is not a table.
3. It is not a chair.

To ask a question with the copula, you need the question word **an**. This word is used with all **verbs** to turn them into questions.

Examples:

An e càr a th' ann?
Is it a car?

An e leabhar a th' ann?
Is it a book?

An e taigh a th' ann?
Is it a house?

Other information:

As with the negative particle, the verb has disappeared again here. This only happens with the copula.

Before some verbs, **an** turns into **am** or **a**.

Exercise 1D. Translate to Gaelic:

1. Is it a pen?
2. Is it a table?
3. Is it a chair?

Important Structure Point

In Gaelic, all **verbs** have a special form that you must use when you want to convey 'indirect' statements (e.g. reported speech). The link word equivalent to English 'that' is *gu*, but it changes to *gur* with the **copula**.

Examples:

Thuirt Calum gur e càr a th' ann.
Calum said that it is a car.

Thuirt Calum gur e leabhar a th' ann.
Calum said that it is a book.

Thuirt Calum gur e taigh a th' ann.
Calum said that it is a house.

Other information:

With some verbs *gu* changes to *gun* or *gum*.

Exercise 1E. Translate to Gaelic:

1. Calum said that it is a pen.
2. Calum said that it is a table.
3. Calum said that it is a chair.

To make a negative indirect statement, the link word used is **nach**.

Examples:

Thuirt Calum nach e càr a th' ann.
Calum said that it is not a car.

Thuirt Calum nach e leabhar a th' ann.
Calum said that it is not a book.

Thuirt Calum nach e taigh a th' ann.

Calum said that it is not a house.

Exercise 1F. Translate to Gaelic:

1. Calum said that it is not a pen.
2. Calum said that it is not a table.
3. Calum said that it is not a chair.

Unit 1 Reading Texts:

Each unit has a set of texts for you to read, in order to practise the Gaelic you are learning in that lesson. In the early units, these texts are really just lists of further examples, although they give slightly more context than the other examples. As the course progresses, you will see the reading texts starting to turn into short passages. Eventually, the passages get slightly longer, and begin to incorporate more and more of the knowledge you have acquired earlier.

Dè tha seo?
'S e càr a th' ann.

Dè tha seo?
'S e taigh a th' ann.

Dè tha seo?
'S e leabhar a th' ann.

Dè tha seo?
'S e peann a th' ann.

Dè tha seo?
'S e bòrd a th' ann.

Dè tha seo?
'S e cathair a th' ann.

Dè tha seo?
'S e càr a th' ann.
Dè thuirt thu?

Thuirt mi gur e càr a th' ann.

Dè tha seo?
'S e bòrd a th' ann.
Dè thuirt thu?
Thuirt mi gur e bòrd a th' ann.

Dè tha seo?
Chan e bòrd a th' ann.
Dè thuirt thu?
Thuirt mi nach e bòrd a th' ann.

Dè tha seo?
Chan e peann a th' ann; 's e cathair a th' ann.
Dè thuirt thu?
Thuirt mi nach e peann a th' ann; thuirt mi gur e cathair a th' ann.

Summary of the copula

QUESTION	An e ... a th' ann?
POSITIVE STATEMENT	'S e ... a th' ann.
NEGATIVE STATEMENT	Chan e ... a th' ann.
INDIRECT STATEMENT	(Thuirt ...) gur e ... a th' ann.
NEGATIVE INDIRECT STATEMENT	(Thuirt ...) nach e ... a th' ann.

Unit 1 Dialogue:

Two students start the Gaelic course and decide to introduce themselves to each other:
MÀIRI: Hi. Is mise Màiri.
NIALL: Halò. Is mise Niall.
A third student joins in:
SEONAIDH: Hi. Is mise Seonaidh.
MÀIRI: Halò. Is mise Màiri, agus is esan Niall.
Seonaidh had been talking to another student. He introduces her to the group now:
SEONAIDH: Seo Mairead.
MAIREAD: Halò!

UNIT 2: 'TO BE' (2)

Technical Terms Used in this Unit

clause   A clause is a meaningful part of a sentence which contains a verb. A **main clause** can stand alone as a sentence in its own right, because it contains a **finite verb**. A **subordinate clause** must be joined to a main clause, as it does not contain a finite verb. This is a main clause: 'The university is closed.' This is a subordinate clause: 'because it is Christmas time.' The first one can stand alone as a sentence without any help, but the second one cannot. You could join the two of them together to make a two-clause sentence: 'The university is closed because it is Christmas time.'

substantive   The substantive verb is the verb 'to be' which joins a noun or pronoun with a verb or another part of speech that is not a noun.

subject   The subject of the sentence is the person or thing that performs the action of the verb. In this sentence, the old lady is the **subject**: 'The old lady eats the cat.' Notice that the **subject** in grammatical terms is not necessarily the topic or theme of the sentence: the word **subject** has a different meaning in grammar.

complement   The complement of a sentence is everything else apart from the verb and the subject.

adjective   An adjective is a word that describes a noun: *big*, *small*, *clever*, etc.

Faclan an Latha ... Your Daily Dose of Vocabulary

Verbs
ag obair	*working*
ag ithe	*eating*
ag òl	*drinking*

Adjectives
sgìth	*tired*
trang	*busy*
toilichte	*happy*

Pronouns
mi	*I, me*	**sinn**	*we, us*
thu	*you*	**sibh**	*you*
e	*he, him, it*	**iad**	*they, them*
i	*she, her, it*		

You will have noticed in Unit 1 that the verb in Gaelic tends to come at the start of the sentence:

'S e càr a th' ann.

Even when we made more complex sentences with two **clauses**, each **clause** started with a verb:

Thuirt Calum gur e càr a th' ann.

This is one of the features of Celtic languages. In Unit 2, you will see this happening with another verb.

'To be' (2)

Tha mi sgìth	I'm tired	Tha mi ag obair	I'm working
Tha mi trang	I'm busy	Tha mi ag ithe	I'm eating
Tha mi toilichte	I'm happy	Tha mi ag òl	I'm drinking

The second verb 'to be' in Gaelic is called the **substantive**. The part used to form positive statements is *tha*, which means 'am', 'is' and 'are'. You use the **substantive** to make descriptive statements and sentences that do not involve joining two nouns.

Examples:

Tha Màiri beag.
Mary is small.

Tha Eilidh Chaimbeul mòr.
Helen Campbell is big.

Tha thu trang.
You are busy.

The personal pronouns:

mi	*I, me*	sinn	*we, us*
thu	*you*	sibh	*you*
e	*he, him, it*	iad	*they, them*
i	*she, her, it*		

The basic word order of a Gaelic sentence is Verb-**Subject**-**Complement**. The **subject** of a sentence can be either a noun or a pronoun (this is also true of sentences in English).

Other information:

In Unit 1, you saw slightly different versions of some of the personal pronouns. These (***mise***, ***esan***, ***ise***) were emphatic versions of the pronouns, which you will see again in more detail soon.

Exercise 2A. Translate to Gaelic:

1. I am big.
2. You are small.
3. We are busy.
4. They are happy.

Exercise 2B. Translate to English:

1. Tha Calum sgìth.
2. Tha Eilidh trang.
3. Tha iad ag obair.
4. Tha sinn ag òl.

As you can see, the noun or pronoun that is acting as the **subject** of the sentence comes immediately after the verb:

Tha [SUBJECT] sgìth/trang/toilichte/ag obair/ag ithe/ag òl, etc.

Another way to think of this is to consider the verb and the **subject** as a unit that work together: they *must* appear together, always in the same order in basic statements:

VERB-SUBJECT

> ### Other Information:
> Women's names and girls' names are feminine nouns. Therefore, when a woman or girl's surname follows her first name, the surname is lenited if possible, acquiring an *h*: Eilidh Chaimbeul. You will learn about lenition in a later unit. The surname element ***mac*** means 'son of'. Obviously, a woman is not likely to be anyone's son. The female equivalent of ***mac*** is ***nic***, which means 'daughter of'.

Recap:
- There are two verbs 'to be' in Gaelic: the copula (***is***) and the **substantive** (***tha***);
- You use ***is*** to join two nouns or a noun and a pronoun;
- You use ***tha*** to join the subject with a complement other than a noun/pronoun.

It is very important, therefore, that you should be able to recognise nouns and pronouns and distinguish them from other classes of words. If you are unclear on this, you should revise these terms and make an effort to improve your understanding. Ask the teacher for help if necessary.

> **Other information:**
>
> There are two words used for 'you' in Gaelic. When talking to one person you know well, or when talking to somebody younger than you, use **thu**. When talking to somebody you have just met or somebody who is at an emotional distance from you, use **sibh**. You also use **sibh** when talking to more than one person, even when you are just talking to two small children. Many speakers also use **sibh** to address their parents or other relatives of an older generation.

Exercise 2C. Translate the following to Gaelic:

1. It is a book.
2. He is busy.
3. Eilidh is working.
4. It is a pen.

> **Other information:**
>
> In this unit, you have been introduced to three verbal nouns (**ag obair**, **ag ithe**, **ag òl**). Verbal nouns are cross-over words that can function as both verbs and nouns. In English, these words end in *–ing*, as in 'running', 'eating', 'thinking'. In Gaelic, they often appear with a small word before them. Here, you can see them with the word **ag**, which indicates that the action of the verb is in progress. Verbal nouns act like any other **complement**.

The negative form of the **substantive** verb is ***chan eil***.

Examples:

Chan eil Màiri beag.
Mary is not small.

Chan eil Eilidh Chaimbeul mòr.
Helen Campbell is not big.

Chan eil thu trang.
You are not busy.

Exercise 2D. Translate to Gaelic:

1. I am not big.
2. You are not small.
3. We are not busy.
4. They are not happy.

The question form of the **substantive** verb is ***a bheil***.

Examples:

A bheil Màiri beag?
Is Mary small?

A bheil Eilidh Chaimbeul mòr?
Is Helen Campbell big?

A bheil thu trang?
Are you busy?

Exercise 2E. Translate to Gaelic:

1. Am I big?
2. Are you small?
3. Are we busy?
4. Are they happy?

To make indirect statements with the **substantive** verb, use ***gu bheil***.

Examples:

Thuirt mi gu bheil Màiri beag.
I said that Mary is small.

Thuirt mi gu bheil Eilidh Chaimbeul mòr.
I said that Helen Campbell is big.

Thuirt mi gu bheil thu trang.
I said that you are busy.

Other information:

In informal conversation, you may notice that **gu bheil** is often elided, so that it sounds a bit like **g' eil**. Similarly, **a bheil** can sound like **bheil** or even **'eil**. In more formal or old-fashioned writing, on the other hand, **a bheil** sometimes appears as **am bheil** or **am beil**.

To make negative indirect statements with the **substantive** verb, use **nach eil**.

Examples:

Thuirt mi nach eil Màiri beag.
I said that Mary is not small.

Thuirt mi nach eil Eilidh Chaimbeul mòr.
I said that Helen Campbell is not big.

Thuirt mi nach eil thu trang.
I said that you are not busy.

Exercise 2F. Translate to English:

1. Thuirt sinn gu bheil thu ag obair.
2. A bheil thu sgìth?
3. Thuirt Ruaraidh gur e peann a th' ann.
4. Chan eil sinn trang.
5. Chan eil i ag ithe.
6. Tha mi toilichte gu bheil thu ag obair.

Notice that the link words for indirect statements are not just used for 'reported speech'. In number 6 in the above exercise, they are used to link two clauses just like the English word 'that'.

Unit 2 Reading Texts:

Tha mi sgìth
Tha thu sgìth
Tha e sgìth
Tha i sgìth
Tha sinn sgìth
Tha sibh sgìth
Tha iad sgìth

Tha mi ag obair
Tha thu ag obair
Tha e ag obair
Tha i ag obair
Tha sinn ag obair
Tha sibh ag obair
Tha iad ag obair

Tha mi toilichte.
Dè thuirt thu?
Thuirt mi gu bheil mi toilichte.

Tha i sgìth.
Dè thuirt thu?
Thuirt mi gu bheil i sgìth.

Chan eil sinn toilichte.
Dè thuirt thu?
Thuirt mi nach eil sinn toilichte.

Chan eil sinn toilichte.
Dè thuirt sibh?
Thuirt sinn nach eil sinn toilichte.

A bheil thu trang?
A bheil thu sgìth?
A bheil thu toilichte?

A bheil Calum trang?

Chan eil iad toilichte.
Chan eil Mairead toilichte.

Is mise Iain. Tha mi ag obair.
Is ise Mairead. Chan eil i sgìth.
Seo Seonaidh. Tha e trang.
Sin Màiri. Tha i ag ithe.

Summary of the substantive verb

Question	A bheil ... ?
Positive Statement	Tha ...
Negative Statement	Chan eil ...
Indirect Statement	(Thuirt ...) gu bheil ...
Negative Indirect statement	(Thuirt ...) nach eil ...

Unit 2 Dialogue:

The teacher asks people their names:

TIDSEAR: Dè an t-ainm a th' ort?
MÀIRI: Is mise Màiri.
TIDSEAR: Agus cò tha sin?
MÀIRI: Is esan Seonaidh.
TIDSEAR: Dè an t-ainm a th' ort?
CALUM: Is mise Calum.
TIDSEAR: Dè thuirt thu?
CALUM: Thuirt mi gur mise Calum.
TIDSEAR: Agus cò tha sin?
CALUM: Is ise Mairead.
TIDSEAR: Madainn mhath a Mhairead.
MAIREAD: Madainn mhath.

UNIT 3: 'YES' AND 'NO'

Technical Terms Used in this Unit

positive — In Gaelic grammar, each verb has a form which is used for making affirmative statements and for answering questions affirmatively. We often refer to this is as the **positive** form of the verb. With the substantive, the positive form is ***tha***.

negative — The negative form of the verb is used for making negative statements and for answering questions as a 'no'. With the substantive, the negative form is ***chan eil***.

tense — The **tense** of a verb is the form it takes to show <u>when</u> the action happens. In this example, the verb is in the past tense: "I <u>walked</u> home." In this example, the verb is in the present tense: "I <u>walk</u> home."

conjunction — A **conjunction** is a 'joining' word. Conjunctions let two or more words join up together. There are several different kinds of conjunctions, but they all perform the basic function of 'joining'. The most basic ones in English are 'and', 'but' and 'or'.

attributive — An adjective acts **attributively** when it is attached to a noun and is giving a description of that noun: 'the <u>big</u> pencil' – here, 'big' is **attributive**, because it is telling us about the pencil's attributes.

predicative — An adjective acts **predicatively** when it completes the sense of the sentence (i.e. the sentence would not mean anything without the adjective): 'the shop is <u>busy</u> today' – here, 'busy' is **predicative**, because it is the **predicate** of the sentence (missing it out would make the sentence meaningless).

Faclan an Latha ... Your Daily Dose of Vocabulary

Numbers

neoni	*zero*	**còig**	*five*
aon	*one*	**sia**	*six*
dhà / dà	*two*	**seachd**	*seven*
trì	*three*	**ochd**	*eight*
ceithir	*four*	**naoi**	*nine*
		deich	*ten*

Adjectives

beag — *small*
mòr — *big*

Conjunctions

agus — *and*
ach — *but*

So far, you have encountered the two verbs in Gaelic which are equivalent to the English verb 'to be'. You know how to make a positive statement, a negative statement, ask a question and make an indirect statement with each of these verbs. In this unit, you will learn how to answer questions.

Like other Celtic languages, Gaelic lacks single, separate words for 'yes' and 'no'. Instead, you must recognise which verb was used in the question and then answer with either a **positive** or **negative** form of that verb. This is true for almost every situation, with every verb, in every **tense**. It is therefore essential that you get used to doing it as soon as possible and keep practising it.

As it happens, you already know the words that you need in order to be able to answer questions with the two verbs 'to be'. If the question begins with *a bheil*, you answer *tha* for 'yes' or *chan eil* for 'no'.

Examples:

A bheil Màiri beag?
Is Mary small?

Tha.
Yes.

A bheil thu sgìth?
Are you tired?

Chan eil.
No.

A bheil Dòmhnall ag obair?
Is Donald working?

Tha.
Yes.

A bheil thu ag ithe?
Are you eating?

Chan eil.
No.

It is very important to note that *tha* is NOT 'the Gaelic word for yes' and *chan eil* is

NOT 'the Gaelic word for no'. **Tha** is used for 'yes' only when the question is *a bheil*, and **chan eil** is used for 'no' only when the question is *a bheil*.

Exercise 3A. Translate to English:

1. A bheil thu trang? Tha.
2. A bheil i ag òl? Chan eil.
3. A bheil Calum sgìth? Tha.

Exercise 3B. Translate to Gaelic:

1. Are we happy? No.
2. Is Donald big? Yes.
3. Are you working? Yes.

Other information:

Previously, we have used adjectives **attributively**, but you can also use them **predicatively**. To say 'it is a big car', you say *'s e càr mòr a th' ann*, but to say 'the car is big', you say *tha an càr mòr*. In the first example, the adjective is part of a phrase along with the noun, and is acting **attributively**; in the second, the adjective is finishing the sense of the sentence and is acting **predicatively**.

Sometimes a person giving an answer will back up their 'yes' or 'no' with further clarification by giving a positive statement:

Examples:

A bheil thu trang?
Are you busy?

Tha, tha mi trang.
Yes, I am busy.

A bheil i sgìth?

Is she tired?

Chan eil, chan eil i sgìth.
No, she is not tired.

Notice that this kind of further clarification results in the verb being repeated, because of the two jobs it is doing (i.e. it is answering 'yes' or 'no' and also forming a sentence).

With the copula, the question form is **an e**. When a question begins **an e**, the 'yes' answer is **'s e** and the 'no' answer is **chan e**. Again, you will recognise these as the **positive** and **negative** forms of the copula: the same forms used for making statements.

Examples:

An e peann a th' ann?
Is it a pen?

'S e.
Yes.

An e càr a th' ann?
Is it a car?

Chan e.
No.

Exercise 3C. Translate to Gaelic:

1. Is it a table? No.
2. Is it a house? Yes.
3. Is it a chair? No.

> **Other information:**
>
> Remember that **'s e** is a shortened form of **is e**. The word **is** is the copula, the verb 'to be' which is used to link two nouns or a noun and a pronoun. The word **e** is the 3rd person singular masculine pronoun, meaning 'he' or 'it'.

The **conjunctions** *agus* and *ach* are used very much in the same way as their English equivalents: they effectively join two elements together.

Examples:

Tha Iain agus Dòmhnall mòr.
Iain and Donald are big.

Tha an taigh mòr ach tha an leabhar beag.
The house is big but the book is small.

Tha Seònaid ag obair ach chan eil i trang.
Janet is working but she isn't busy.

Unit 3 Reading Texts:

A bheil i beag?
Tha

A bheil i beag?
Chan eil

A bheil thu trang?
Tha

A bheil thu trang?
Chan eil

A bheil mi toilichte?
Tha

A bheil mi toilichte?
Chan eil

A bheil Calum ag obair?
Tha

A bheil Calum ag obair?
Chan eil

A bheil i beag?
Tha, tha i beag.

A bheil i beag?
Chan eil, chan eil i beag.

A bheil i beag?
Chan eil; tha i mòr.

A bheil thu trang?
Tha, tha mi trang.

A bheil thu toilichte?
Chan eil; tha mi trang ag obair!

A bheil thu sgìth?
Tha; tha mi sgìth ach toilichte.

A bheil Iain trang?
Chan eil, ach tha e sgìth.

A bheil i ag ithe?
Chan eil, ach tha i ag òl.

Tha mi ag ithe agus ag òl.
Tha mi trang agus toilichte.
Tha mi sgìth ag obair.
Tha mi trang ag obair.
Tha Mairead trang ach tha i toilichte.

An e càr a th' ann?
'S e.

An e càr a th' ann?
Chan e.

An e bòrd a th' ann?
'S e.

An e bòrd a th' ann?
Chan e.

An e bòrd mòr a th' ann?
'S e.

An e bòrd mòr a th' ann?
Chan e.

An e bòrd mòr a th' ann?
Chan e; 's e bòrd a th' ann, ach chan eil e mòr.

An e bòrd mòr a th' ann?
Chan e; 's e bòrd beag a th' ann.

An e taigh mòr a th' ann?
'S e.

An e taigh mòr a th' ann?
Chan e; chan e taigh a th' ann.

An e taigh mòr a th' ann?
Chan e; 's e taigh a th' ann, ach tha e beag.

Summary:

Question form:	'Yes' answer	'No' answer
A bheil ... ?	**Tha**	**Chan eil**
An e ... ?	**'S e**	**Chan e**

Unit 3 Dialogue:

The class begins with some introductions and then they work on identifying things in Gaelic:

TIDSEAR: Latha math! Is mise Sìne. Is mise an tidsear. Ciamar a tha sibh?
MÀIRI: Tha gu math, tapadh leibh. Ciamar a tha sibh fhèin?
TIDSEAR: Tha gu math. Agus, a Chaluim? Ciamar a tha thu?
CALUM: Tha mi glè mhath, tapadh leibh.
TIDSEAR: A Chaluim, ciamar a tha Mairead?
CALUM: Chan eil fhios a'm.

Calum turns to Mairead.

CALUM: A Mhairead, ciamar a tha thu?
MAIREAD: Tha mi gu math.

Calum turns back to the teacher.

CALUM: Tha Mairead gu math.
TIDSEAR: Glè mhath. Cò às a tha thu, a Mhàiri?
MÀIRI: Tha mi à Glaschu.
TIDSEAR: Agus cò às a tha Calum agus Mairead?
MÀIRI: Chan eil fhios a'm.

Màiri turns to Calum and Mairead.

MÀIRI: Cò às a tha sibh?
CALUM: Às Inbhir Nis.
MAIREAD: Leòdhas.

Màiri turns back to the teacher.

MÀIRI: Tha Calum às Inbhir Nis agus tha Mairead à Leòdhas.

There is a brief pause while the teacher takes some objects out of a bag. They turn out to be a little toy house, a little toy car, a pen and a book.

TIDSEAR: A Mhairead, dè tha seo? *She points to the book.*
MAIREAD: 'S e leabhar a th' ann.
TIDSEAR: 'S e. Agus dè tha seo? *She points to the house.*
MAIREAD: 'S e peann a th' ann. *This is the wrong answer.*
TIDSEAR: Chan e. Dè th' ann?
MAIREAD: Tha mi duilich. An e taigh a th' ann?
TIDSEAR: 'S e. Glè mhath!

UNIT 4: 'THE'

Technical Terms Used in this Unit

masculine
: This is just a name for one of the two categories of nouns in Gaelic. These names are inherited from long-standing traditions in the teaching of other languages, and are not very useful in Gaelic – unfortunately, they are the well-established names. 'Male' things do tend to be masculine, but *all* nouns are either masculine or feminine – including things which are clearly neither male nor female.

feminine
: See the gloss above. Famously, the Gaelic word for a woman, 'boireannach', is a masculine noun. Do not mix up **masculine** and **feminine** with 'male' and 'female'.

gender
: This is the name for the two categories, masculine and feminine. When we ask which **gender** a noun is, we are really asking which of the two groups it belongs to.

lenite
: **Lenition** is the process of 'softening' the sound at the beginning of a word. For instance, the /k/ sound changes to /x/ when it is **lenited**. In writing, the change would be from c to ch. **Lenition** is one of the features that mark Gaelic as a Celtic language.

Faclan an Latha ... Your Daily Dose of Vocabulary

Key Phrases and Greetings

madainn mhath	*good morning*	**Ciamar a tha thu?**	*How are you?*
feasgar math	*good afternoon/evening*	**tha gu math**	*I'm well*
latha math	*good day*	**tapadh leat**	*thank you*
oidhche mhath	*goodnight (parting only)*	**chan eil dona**	*not bad*
Dè an t-ainm a th' ort?	*What's your name?*	**tioraidh**	*bye / cheerio*
		tioraidh an-dràsta	*bye for now*

Nouns

uinneag (f)	*window*	**an uinneag**	*the window*
balach (m)	*boy*	**am balach**	*the boy*
caileag (f)	*girl*	**a' chaileag**	*the girl*

Adjectives

math	*good*
dona	*bad*

Numbers

aon-deug	*eleven*
dhà-dheug	*twelve*
trì-deug	*thirteen*
ceithir-deug	*fourteen*
còig-deug	*fifteen*
sia-deug	*sixteen*
seachd-deug	*seventeen*
ochd-deug	*eighteen*
naoi-deug	*nineteen*
fichead	*twenty*

There are two kinds of nouns in Gaelic. They are grouped according to the ways in which they change in certain situations and the ways they affect words around them. We call them **masculine** nouns and **feminine** nouns, but these are slightly misleading terms: they do NOT mean 'male' and 'female'. **Masculine** and **feminine** are just names which language teachers have tended to use for categories of nouns.

The majority of nouns in Gaelic are **masculine**, but many of the very common everyday words are **feminine**. If you ever have to guess which **gender** a noun is, it is a good bet to guess it is masculine. Rather than guessing, though, it is best just to learn the **gender** as soon as you learn a new noun. There are three methods that people usually use to learn **genders**: you can choose the one that suits you best, or use a mixture of all three:

1. Memorise the **gender**; when you first encounter a noun in this course or in a dictionary, it will usually be followed by the letter 'm' or 'f' in brackets. Remember both the meaning of the word and the **gender** together; or
2. Learn the noun together with an adjective (and you will see why in a moment); or
3. Learn the noun together with the definite article (you will see why in a later unit).

Many native speakers of Gaelic will not be able to tell you whether a noun is masculine or feminine, not having learnt these terms. But, if you ask them to say the noun with an adjective, you will find your answer.

Recap of the nouns you know from earlier units:

bòrd (m)   **leabhar (m)**
càr (m)   **peann (m)**
cathair (f)   **taigh (m)**

With their definite articles, these are:

am bòrd
the table

an càr

the car

a' chathair
the chair

an leabhar
the book

am peann
the pen

an taigh
the house

What do you notice about the words, their articles and their genders so far?

When a **feminine** noun is followed by an adjective (and no other words are acting on the noun), the adjective is **lenited**. This means that the sound at the beginning of the adjective is changed ('softened'). We mark this change in the written language by adding the letter 'h'.

cathair mhòr
a big chair

peann mòr
a big pen

uinneag bheag
a small window

bòrd beag
a small table

So, when the adjectives follow the **masculine** nouns (***peann*** and ***bòrd***), they are unchanged, but when they follow the **feminine** nouns (***cathair*** and ***uinneag***), they are **lenited**.

> **Other information:**
>
> This is only true when the adjectives are behaving attributively. When they are behaving predicatively, they are never lenited. We will deal with this in more detail in a later unit.

Further examples, this time with the definite articles:

am balach mòr
the big boy

a' chaileag mhòr
the big girl

am peann math
the good pen

an uinneag mhath
the good window

Exercise 4A. Translate to Gaelic:

1. It is a big chair.
2. Is it a big house?
3. The good boy is working.
4. A little girl is eating.

Exercise 4B. Translate to Gaelic:

1. A little girl and a little boy.
2. The girl is busy, but she is not tired.
3. It is not a good pen.

Important Structural Points

Only certain letters can **lenite**. These are the letters b, c, d, f, g, m, p, s, and t. The letter s cannot **lenite** when it is directly followed by g, m, p or t. Vowels never **lenite**, and the letters l, n and r never show **lenition** by having the h added. The letter h itself also never **lenites**, and it only appears at the beginning of a very few words in Gaelic anyway.

So, when an adjective begins with one of these un**lenitable** letters or combinations of letters, it does not change:

am balach sgìth
the tired boy

a' chaileag sgìth
the tired girl

(Bear this in mind if you are trying to work out a gender by asking one of your native speaker friends to tell you how the noun sounds together with an adjective! Use an adjective that *can* lenite.)

Exercise 4C. Translate to Gaelic:

1. The tired boy and the tired girl.
2. The tired boy is drinking but the tired girl is not happy.
3. Is it a big table? Yes.
4. Is it a good book? No, it is not a good book.

Exercise 4D. Work with a partner.

1. Individually, write down four questions using either ***a bheil*** or ***an e***.
2. Ask your partner the four questions and note down his/her answers (***tha***, ***chan eil***, ***'s e*** or ***chan e***). Of course, both the questions and the answers will be essentially nonsensical, but this is just a language exercise.
3. Swap round and answer your partner's questions.
4. Find another partner and repeat the process.

Exercise 4E. Translate to English:

1. Thuirt mi nach e peann math a th' ann.*
2. Thuirt Màiri gu bheil i ag obair agus gu bheil i sgìth.
3. Thuirt iad nach eil iad ag ithe ach gu bheil iad ag òl.

*It may be helpful to look over the end of Unit 1 again before trying this one.

Unit 4 Reading Texts:

Latha math.
'S e latha math a th' ann.
An e latha math a th' ann?
Chan e latha math a th' ann.

Uinneag bheag.
'S e uinneag bheag a th' ann.
Chan e uinneag bheag a th' ann.

An uinneag bheag.
BUT
Tha an uinneag beag.
A bheil an uinneag beag?
Chan eil an uinneag beag.

Am balach beag.
An e balach beag a th' ann?
'S e.

An e balach beag a th' ann?
Chan e; 's e balach a th' ann, ach tha e mòr.

BUT
A bheil am balach beag?
Tha.

A bheil am balach beag?
Chan eil.

A bheil am balach mòr?
Chan eil; tha e beag.

A bheil am balach mòr?
Chan eil; 's e balach beag a th' ann.

A' chaileag mhòr.
Tha a' chaileag mòr.
A bheil i mòr?
Cò?
A' chaileag? A bheil a' chaileag mòr?
Tha.

Tha a' chaileag mòr.
A bheil i beag?
Cò?
A' chaileag? A bheil a' chaileag beag?
Chan eil; tha mi mòr.

Short Passage: A' Chaileag Mhòr (The Big Girl)

Tha caileag mhòr ann. Tha i trang. Tha i ag obair. Tha balach beag ann. Chan eil e ag obair. Tha am balach ag ithe. Chan eil a' chaileag ag ithe, ach tha i ag òl. Chan eil am balach ag òl, ach tha e toilichte.

Summary:
1. When an adjective is attached to a **masculine** noun and no other words are acting on the noun, the adjective does not change (***balach math***);
2. When an adjective is attached to a **feminine** noun and no other words are acting on the noun, the adjective **lenites** if it begins with a letter that can **lenite** (***caileag mhath***).

Unit 4 Dialogue:

The class continues identifying objects:

TIDSEAR:	Dè an t-ainm a th' ort?
NIALL:	Is mise Niall.
TIDSEAR:	Latha math, a Nèill. Ciamar a tha thu?
NIALL:	Chan eil dona, tapadh leibh.
TIDSEAR:	Cò às a tha thu?
NIALL:	Tha mi às Èirinn.
TIDSEAR:	Seadh. A Nèill, dè tha seo? *She points to a chair.*
NIALL:	'S e cathair bheag a th' ann.
TIDSEAR:	'S e cathair a th' ann, ach a bheil i beag?
NIALL:	Tha.
TIDSEAR:	A Chaluim, dè thuirt Niall?

CALUM:	Thuirt e gur e cathair bheag a th' ann.
TIDSEAR:	Glè mhath. Agus dè tha seo, a Chaluim? *She points to the book.*
CALUM:	'S e leabhar a th' ann.
TIDSEAR:	'S e. An e leabhar mòr a th' ann?
CALUM:	Chan e.
TIDSEAR:	Tha mi duilich. Dè thuirt thu?
CALUM:	Thuirt mi nach e leabhar mòr a th' ann.
TIDSEAR:	B' àilleibh? Thuirt thu gu bheil e mòr?
CALUM:	Thuirt mi **nach eil** e mòr. Thuirt mi **nach e** leabhar mòr a th' ann. 'S e leabhar beag a th' ann.
TIDSEAR:	'S e, ach 's e leabhar math a th' ann.
CALUM:	(*shrugging*) Chan eil fhios a'm.
TIDSEAR:	Dè tha seo, a Mhàiri? *She points to the window.*
MÀIRI:	'S e uinneag a th' ann.
TIDSEAR:	'S e. 'S e sin an unneag. An e uinneag mhòr a th' ann?
MÀIRI:	Chan e. 'S e uinneag bheag a th' ann.
TIDSEAR:	A Mhairead, a bheil an uinneag beag?
MAIREAD:	Chan eil; chan eil i beag.

UNIT 5: SPELLING AND THE PRESENT TENSE

Technical Terms Used in this Unit

periphrastic — Expressed in a 'round-about' way, using a phrase instead of a single word

interrogative — An interrogative is a question-word, such as 'who', 'where' or 'why'.

preposition — A preposition is a word (or sometimes a group of words) that come(s) before a noun or a pronoun and shows how the noun or pronoun relates to other parts of the sentence. Prepositions in English include 'to', 'at', 'by', 'in', 'on', 'under', 'beside', 'from'.

Faclan an Latha ... Your Daily Dose of Vocabulary

Key Words and Phrases

cò às a tha thu / sibh?	where are you from?
tha mi à ...	I'm from ...

Adverbs

an-còmhnaidh	always

Verbs

chuala	heard		
an cuala?	did ... hear?	an tuirt ... ?	did ... say ... ?
cha chuala	didn't hear	cha tuirt ...	... did not say ...

Interrogatives

ciamar?	how?
cò?	who? which?
dè?	what?

Numbers

fichead 's a h-aon	twenty-one
fichead 's a dhà	twenty-two
fichead 's a trì	twenty-three
fichead 's a ceithir	twenty-four
fichead 's a còig	twenty-five
fichead 's a sia	twenty-six
fichead 's a seachd	twenty-seven
fichead 's a h-ochd	twenty-eight
fichead 's a naoi	twenty-nine
fichead 's a deich	thirty
fichead 's a h-aon-deug	thirty-one

Even though Gaelic has very many sounds, it uses a lean alphabet of only 18 letters. In fact, only 17 of these have full 'letter status' and the other one, the letter 'h', is used primarily to mark lenition. The letters in the Gaelic alphabet are:

a, b, c, d, e, f, g, h, i, l, m, n, o, p, r, s, t, u

You will notice that letters familiar to English-speakers, 'j', 'k', 'q' and the letters 'v'-'z' are all missing. The Gaelic writing system has adapted its spelling in a remarkable way that allows the language to express more sounds than most people's English, and yet with fewer letters.

One of the tricks that the Gaelic writing system uses is the grave accent (`). Note that the grave slants from up to down, or is higher on the left than on the right. The grave is mainly used to show that a vowel is long, but it also distinguishes vowel quality in some instances. You will learn more about this in later units. The accent can appear on any of the vowels: à, è, ì, ò, ù. In modern Gaelic writing, the grave is written on both lower case and capital letters: in previous years, most people avoided using accents on capitals (because they had been unavailable on most typewriters).

Other information:

In the past, the letters in Gaelic were named after trees, and they were grouped in a different order from what we normally think of as 'alphabetical order'. Today, they are always presented in the Greek/Latin-derived order familiar to speakers of most languages that use the Latin alphabet. The names of the letters have nowadays become largely similar to the English names, and many speakers simply use the English names when spelling words out loud.

A second trick that Gaelic uses to allow the small number of letters to express a large number of sounds is the system of broad and slender vowels and consonants. The vowels 'a', 'o' and 'u' are considered to be broad and the vowels 'e' and 'i' are considered to be slender. You will learn more about this in later units, but for now remember the age-old Gaelic spelling rule:

caol ri caol is leathann ri leathann
slender to slender and broad to broad

From a spelling perspective, what this means is that, if a consonant is preceded by a broad vowel, any vowel that comes after that consonant must be broad; if a consonant is preceded by a slender vowel, any vowel that comes after that consonant must be slender.

The third main trick that Gaelic uses to let its small number of letters spell out a large number of sounds is the deployment of the letter 'h' to show lenition. You already know that some situations cause a sound change in Gaelic consonants (a 'softening') and that that change is usually marked by adding the letter 'h'. We know that the letters b, c, d, f, g, m, p, s, and t can lenite. Simply by adding 'h', the spelling system adds several more sounds to the language. (English does something similar – think of 'sh', 'ch' etc.)

The Present Tense

Apart from a few relics in phrases and sayings, there are only two verbs in Gaelic which have a present tense. These are the two verbs you already know: the substantive ***tha*** ('is', 'am', 'are') and the copula ***is*** ('is', 'am', 'are'). Therefore, to express anything in the present, you must use one of these two verbs. The most common way of expressing present tense actions is to use the substantive verb and a verbal noun.

Examples:

Tha mi ag obair.
I am working. (Or) I work.

Tha i ag ithe.
She is eating. (Or) She eats.

Other information:

In a later unit, you will learn another way of expressing habitual actions, but it is not uncommon to use ***tha*** for this.

Important Structural Point

Note that you CANNOT use the copula in this way. The copula is for defining, identifying and emphasising. It is not used for describing (except emphatically) or explaining.

Further examples:

Chuala mi gu bheil Eilidh trang ag obair an-diugh.
I heard that Eilidh is busy working today.

Chuala mi gu bheil Eilidh an-còmhnaidh ag obair.
I heard that Eilidh always works / is always working.

An tuirt thu gu bheil thu trang?
Did you say that you are busy?

Thuirt Dòmhnall nach eil e sgìth.
Donald said that he is not tired.

Exercise 5A. Work with two other people.

1. Individually, compose five simple sentences that you are confident are in correct Gaelic (e.g. <u>tha mi ag ithe</u>);
2. Introduce yourself to one partner (Person 2) in Gaelic;
3. Read out one of your sentences to Person 2;
4. Introduce Person 2 to the third partner (Person 3) (– remember how to introduce someone else?);
5. Person 2 uses the indirect form to report to Person 3 what you just said.
6. Repeat the process for all your sentences and in as many permutations as you can think of.

Example:

1. I write down:

Tha mi trang.

2. **Me:** Hai. Is mise Bill. Ciamar a tha thu?
   Person 2: Hai Bill. Is mise Clare. Tha gu math, tapadh leat.
3. **Me:** Tha mi trang.
4. **Me:** Hai. Is mise Bill. Seo Clare.
5. **Person 2 (to Person 3):** Thuirt Bill gu bheil e trang.
6. **Person 2:** Hai. Is mise Clare. Ciamar a tha thu?
   etc.

Exercise 5B. Translate to Gaelic

1. The car is small.
2. The car is not small.
3. Is the car small?
4. It is a small car.
5. It is not a small car.
6. Is it a small car?
7. Iain said that the car is small.
8. Iain said that the car is not small.
9. Did Iain say that the car is small?
10. Iain did not say that the car is small.
11. Did Iain say that it is a small car?
12. Did Iain say that it is not a small car?

More on lenition

Some words cause a following word to be lenited, just by being present. **Intensifiers** like *glè*, *sàr* and *fìor* all cause lenition of a following adjective:

glè mhòr
very big

sàr mhath
excellent

fìor bheag
very little

Some **prepositions** cause lenition of the noun that follows them. The ones that cause lenition are *do*, *de*, *bho*, *o*, *fo*, *mu*, *a*, *tro*, *ro*. You will be learning these soon.

Unit 5 Reading Texts:
A Further Example of Exercise 5A

Sorcha writes:
Tha Iain trang
Tha mi ag obair
Chan eil mi toilichte

Ruaraidh writes:
Tha mi toilichte
Chan e bòrd mòr a th' ann
Chan e latha math a th' ann
Tha mi sgìth

Tormod writes:
Chan eil Mairead ag ithe
Tha an tidsear math
'S e peann mòr a th' ann

SORCHA: Halò. Is mise Sorcha.
RUARAIDH: Latha math. Is mise Ruaraidh.
SORCHA: Ciamar a tha thu, a Ruaraidh?
RUARAIDH: Tha gu math, tapadh leat. Ciamar a tha thu fhèin?
SORCHA: Tha gu math. *Looking at her list*. Tha Iain trang.
Sorcha turns to the student on her right.
SORCHA: Hai. Is mise Sorcha. Seo Ruaraidh.
RUARAIDH: Thuirt Sorcha gu bheil Iain trang.
TORMOD: Hai. Is mise Tormod.
SORCHA: Halò, a Thormoid. Ciamar a tha thu?
TORMOD: Tha gu math tapadh leat.
RUARAIDH: (*looking at his list*) Chan e bòrd mòr a th' ann.
TORMOD: (*to Sorcha*) Thuirt Ruaraidh nach e bòrd mòr a th' ann.
SORCHA: Chan e.
TORMOD: (*looking at his list*) Tha an tidsear math.
SORCHA: (*to Ruaraidh*) Thuirt Tormod gu bheil an tidsear math.

Summary of present tense structure:
Tha [SUBJECT] [COMPLEMENT]
Chan eil [SUBJECT] [COMPLEMENT]
A bheil [SUBJECT] [COMPLEMENT]?
... gu bheil [SUBJECT] [COMPLEMENT]
... nach eil [SUBJECT] [COMPLEMENT]

Apart from the copula, no other verbs have a present tense, so they all rely on the substantive verb and this **periphrastic** construction.

Unit 5 Dialogue:

The class has a short break, so the students get to know each other a bit better.

NIALL: Cò às a tha thu, a Mhairead?
MAIREAD: Tha mi à Leòdhas, ach tha mi a' fuireach ann an Obar Dheathain a-nis. Thuirt thu gu bheil thu às Èirinn. Càit ann an Èirinn?
NIALL: Tha mi à Mayo.
MAIREAD: Agus càit a bheil thu a' fuireach an-dràsta?
NIALL: Tha mi a' fuireach ann an Dùn Dèagh an-dràsta.

Niall sneezes.

MAIREAD: A bheil thu gu math?
NIALL: Chan eil: tha an cnatan orm.
MAIREAD: Obh obh!

Meanwhile, Calum is talking to Màiri.

CALUM: Tha an tidsear math.
MÀIRI: Tha. Tha i glè mhath.
CALUM: Càit a bheil thu a' fuireach, a Mhàiri?
MÀIRI: Ann an Obar Dheathain, ann an Rosemount.
CALUM: A bheil? Tha mi fhèin a' fuireach ann an Rosemount.

They agree to meet to practise their Gaelic.

MÀIRI: Dè an àireamh fòn a th' agad?
CALUM: Neoni, a seachd, a seachd, a ceithir, a còig, a h-aon, a dhà, a trì, a ceithir, a còig, a sia. Agus dè an àireamh fòn a th' agad fhèin?
MÀIRI: Neoni, a seachd, a h-ochd, a h-aon, a naoi, a h-ochd, a seachd, a sia, a còig, a ceithir, a trì.

UNIT 6: MASCULINE NOMINATIVE

Technical Terms Used in this Unit

case
: The **case** of a noun is the form it takes in a particular situation. For instance, if the noun is combined with another noun, it may change. In English, when we add the apostrophe and <u>s</u> to a noun or name, we say that the noun or name is in the **genitive** case, because it is showing possession: *Bob's pen*. In some languages, **cases** can have both singular and plural forms. For instance, in English, the position of the apostrophe in the genitive shows whether the noun is singular or plural. Which of the underlined nouns below is plural?

   The <u>boy's</u> pens
   The <u>boys'</u> pens

vocative
: This is the form a person's name takes when you are talking directly to him/her.

genitive
: This is the form a noun takes when it is showing possession or close relationship to another noun (such as *the boy's car* in English).

dative
: This is the form a noun takes when it follows a word like 'in', 'on', 'at', 'by', 'near', etc.

nominative
: This is the form a noun takes when none of the above contexts apply – i.e. the form the noun takes when you look it up in the dictionary.

subject
: The subject of the sentence is the person or thing that performs the action of the verb. In this sentence, <u>the old lady</u> is the **subject**: 'The old lady eats the cat.' Notice that the **subject** in grammatical terms is not necessarily the topic or theme of the sentence: the word **subject** has a different meaning in grammar.

object
: The object of the sentence is the person or thing that receives the action of the verb. In the sentence above, <u>the cat</u> is the **object**, because the verb <u>eats</u> is happening to <u>the cat</u>.

adverb
: An **adverb** tells you more about how, where or when something is happening. Most people know that the *–ly* words are **adverbs** in English – *quickly, hungrily, happily*, etc. Other **adverbs** include words and phrases

like *inside, upstairs, always, often, never, every week, forwards,* etc.

Faclan an Latha ... Your Daily Dose of Vocabulary

Key Words and Phrases

Dè do chor?	*How Are You? (informal)*
Deagh chor	*I'm well*
Cor math	*I'm well*
Droch chor	*I'm in bad form*

Prepositions

do	*to*
bho	*from*

Adverbs

dùinte	*closed, shut*
fosgailte	*open*
làn	*full*
falamh	*empty*

Numbers

dà fhichead	*forty*
dà fhichead 's a h-aon	*forty-one*
lethcheud	*fifty*
lethcheud 's a h-aon	*fifty-one*
trì fichead	*sixty*
trì fichead 's a h-aon	*sixty-one*
trì fichead 's a deich	*seventy*
ceithir fichead	*eighty*
ceithir fichead 's a dhà-dheug	*ninety-two*
ceud	*one hundred*

> **Other information:**
>
> Sometimes a noun or a phrase or a past participle can act as an **adverb**, depending on the context. In the vocabulary today, you have two past participles that are doing the job of **adverbs**. Do you know which two they are?

It is very important that you learn the genders of nouns as you go along. For many people, it is tempting to avoid bothering with the gender: you may feel that, as long as you learn the basic meaning of the word, that will be enough. Unfortunately, if you take this approach, you will soon discover that you cannot properly use the nouns you have been learning. This is because the definite article (the word for 'the') changes depending on three things: (1) the gender of the noun, (2) the **case** the noun is in, and (3) whether the noun is singular or plural. In this unit, we begin exploring the Gaelic **cases**.

Gaelic has four **cases**. They have traditionally been known as **nominative**, **dative**, **genitive** and **vocative**.

In this unit and the next one, we tackle the **nominative** singular.

> **Other information:**
>
> The nominative case is badly named in modern Gaelic, as it covers both the subject and the object and therefore carries out the usual job of an accusative case, too.

With indefinite nouns, the **nominative** singular is incredibly easy: this is the form that the noun takes when you look it up in the dictionary and it is the form in which you will almost certainly learn nearly all the nouns you ever meet in the language. For the nouns you already know, the indefinite (i.e. no word for 'the') **nominative** singular is:

balach (m)
bòrd (m)
caileag (f)
càr (m)
cathair (f)
ainm (m)
feasgar (m)

latha (m)
leabhar (m)
madainn (f)
oidhche (f)
peann (m)
taigh (m)
uinneag (f)

So, you already know the indefinite **nominative** singular for both masculine and feminine nouns – well done!

If you had not yet learned the genders, this is a perfect opportunity: you have a handy list here.

Exercise 6A:
Look through your workbooks at the first week's work and pick out any other nouns. What is the indefinite **nominative** singular of these other nouns?

With definite nouns (i.e. when you add a word for 'the'), the **nominative** singular is different depending on whether the noun is masculine or feminine.

Masculine Nominative Singular

The definite article (the word for 'the') takes three different forms with masculine singular nouns in the **nominative**: am, an t-, or an. The form the article takes depends on the initial letter of the noun. This is the pattern:

am   when the noun begins with b, f, m or p
an t- when the noun begins with a vowel
an   when the noun begins with any other letter

If you say the word am followed by the nouns you know that begin with b, f, m or p, you will notice that they flow together well. This is because am leaves the lips together, and the lips are used to form each of these four letters, too. These are the masculine nouns you already know, together with their definite articles:

am balach
am bòrd
an càr
an t-ainm
am feasgar
an latha
an leabhar
am peann
an taigh

From now on, when you are learning your daily dose of vocabulary, pay close attention to the gender of the noun (marked by the letter m or f), and also take note of the noun with its article on the right-hand side.

Exercise 6B:

Here are some more useful masculine nouns that will be coming up in your workbooks in the next two weeks. Write them down with their definite articles:

1. doras
2. baga
3. biadh
4. aran
5. uisge
6. gille
7. rathad
8. lagh
9. cuspair
10. cànan
11. bràthair
12. cù

If you are keen to know what they mean, flick ahead in your books or look them up in a dictionary (sometimes you remember vocabulary better when you have to look it up for yourself).

> **Other information:**
>
> The word *lagh* can actually be both masculine and feminine, depending on where the speaker comes from. There are only a few words in the language like this. In most cases, words that can be both masculine and feminine used to be neuter when the language had a third gender back in the distant past.

There are some clues that you can use to help you guess the gender of the noun, just in case you have foolishly neglected to learn it as you went along. The first and most useful clue of all is that the great bulk of nouns in Gaelic are masculine. Therefore, if you guess masculine, you will probably be right more times than you will be wrong. The second useful clue is that nouns that have broad consonants at the end tend to be masculine (think of **doras**, **biadh**, **aran**, **rathad**, **cànan** above, but notice that this is not always true, as we also have **cuspair** and we have several nouns that end in vowels). If a noun ends in –**an**, it is usually masculine. Job titles and nationalities are usually masculine. The days of the week and all four seasons are masculine nouns (but the months are a mixture of both masculine and feminine). We will come across some other clues in the next few units.

Exercise 6C. Translate to Gaelic:

1. The door is open.
2. Is the bag empty?
3. I heard that the house is full.
4. He said that the road is busy.
5. They heard that the door is closed.

Exercise 6D. Translate to English:

1. Tha an t-aran math.
2. A bheil an gille beag?
3. Chuala mi gu bheil an doras dùinte.
4. Cha tuirt mi gu bheil an taigh falamh.

Exercise 6E. Match the correct articles and nouns:

~~an~~, an, an, an, an, an, an, an, an, am, am, am, am, am, am, an t-, an t-, an t-

cuspair, ~~doras~~, balach, gille, aran, taigh, lagh, baga, bòrd, càr, uisge, rathad, cù, latha, peann, feasgar, ainm, biadh

an doras, ...

....

....

Unit 6 Reading Texts:

Balach
Tha balach an seo
Tha am balach an seo

'S e balach a th' ann
Is esan am balach

'S e balach mòr a th' ann
Is esan am balach mòr

Short Passage: Am Balach aig an Oilthigh (The Boy at the University)

(A short glossary follows this text)

'S e latha math a th' ann. Tha balach aig an oilthigh. 'S e Gòrdan an t-ainm a th' air. 'S e balach mòr, toilichte a th' ann an Gòrdon. Ach tha Gòrdon glè thrang ag obair. Tha e ag obair aig bòrd. Tha leabhar agus peann air a' bhòrd. Tha Gòrdon ag ithe aran agus ag òl uisge. 'S e leabhar Gàidhlig a th' air a' bhòrd. 'S e Gàidhlig an cuspair a tha Gòrdon a' dèanamh aig an oilthigh. 'S e cànan math a th' ann an Gàidhlig.

Aig: at
Air: on
Oilthigh: university
A' dèanamh: doing, making

Summary of masculine singular nominative:

An adjective qualifying the noun does not lenite	
The article will be:	... when the noun begins with:
am	b, f, m, p
an t-	a, e, i, o, u
an	c, d, g, h, l, n, r, s, t

Unit 6 Dialogue:

ANNA-MÀIRI: Hai. Dè do chor, a Ghòrdan?
GÒRDAN: Hai, Anna-Màiri. Deagh chor, ach tha mi trang. Dè do chor fhèin?
ANNA-MÀIRI: Tha mise gu math. Chuala mi gu bheil thu a' dèanamh Gàidhlig san oilthigh a-nis. A bheil sin ceart?
GÒRDAN: Tha. 'S e sin an cuspair a tha mi a' dèanamh. Tha Gàidhlig glè mhath.
ANNA-MÀIRI: Tha. Agus càit a bheil thu a' fuireach an-dràsta?
GÒRDAN: Tha mi a' fuireach ann an Obar Dheathain. Càit a bheil thu fhèin a' fuireach?
ANNA-MÀIRI: Ann an Glaschu. Tha mi ag obair ann an Glaschu.
GÒRDAN: Tha mi duilich – dè thuirt thu?
ANNA-MÀIRI: Thuirt mi gu bheil mi ag obair ann an Glaschu.
GÒRDAN: O, ceart. Dè an cuspair a tha thu a' dèanamh an sin?
ANNA-MÀIRI: Tha mi a' dèanamh Lagh.
GÒRDAN: Lagh? A bheil sin ceart?
ANNA-MÀIRI: Tha. Tha e math.

San: in the
Ceart: right, correct

UNIT 7: FEMININE NOMINATIVE

Technical Terms Used in this Unit

eclipsis   The phenomenon of a sound from a preceding word taking over the sound at the beginning of the next word. Eclipsis, like lenition, can make words sound as if they start with a completely different letter.

Faclan an Latha ... Your Daily Dose of Vocabulary

Nouns

obair (f)	*work, job*	**an obair**	*the work, the job*
aimsir (f)	*weather*	**an aimsir**	*the weather*
Gàidhlig (f)	*Gaelic*	**a' Ghàidhlig**	*Gaelic (until fairly recently, almost everyone used the article when talking about the language)*
Beurla (f)	*English*	**a' Bheurla**	*English (note that **Beurla** only means the language – it can never be used as the national adjective)*
leabaidh (f)	*bed*	**an leabaidh**	*the bed*
iris (f)	*magazine*	**an iris**	*the magazine*
oifis (f)	*office*	**an oifis**	*the office*
sràid (f)	*street*	**an t-sràid**	*the street*
sgoil (f)	*school*	**an sgoil**	*(the) school*
feòil (f)	*meat*	**an fheòil**	*the meat*

Adverbs

an-diugh — *today*

Prepositions

de — *of, off*
tro — *through*
mu — *about*

Feminine Nominative Singular

The feminine version of the nominative singular is slightly more complex than the masculine version, for two reasons:

(1) There are four possible ways for the article and start of the noun to behave;
(2) An adjective lenites when it follows a feminine noun.

> How many ways can the article and start of the noun behave if the noun is masculine?

The three forms of the article with feminine nouns in the nominative are: a', an and an t-. The fourth 'behaviour' pattern is that when an comes before a noun that starts with an f, the noun is lenited. The pattern is as follows:

a'   when the noun begins with b, c, g, m or p. **The noun lenites**.
an   when the noun begins with f. **The noun lenites**.
an t- when the noun begins with sa, se, si, so, su, sl, sn, sr.
an   when the noun begins with any other letter

Notice that I have not arranged the 's' combinations in alphabetical order. This is to emphasise that another way of listing them would be: s + vowel, sl, sn, sr. It may be easier or quicker for you to memorise it like that. The t- joins onto the noun, with no gap in spelling. It also joins on with no gap in pronunciation, and it cancels out the 's' sound (so the word sounds as if it starts with a t). We call this process **eclipsis**, and it is one of the identifying features of Gaelic and the other Celtic languages.

> Can you think of any reason why **eclipsis** might cause problems when you are learning Gaelic?

There are four other combinations with s at the beginning of a word in Gaelic: sg, sm, sp and st. You may remember from an earlier unit that these combinations NEVER lenite.

Here are the feminine nouns you already know:

caileag
cathair
madainn
oidhche
uinneag

Exercise 7A. Following the pattern above, and without look back over the vocabulary lists, put these nouns with their definite articles.

Remember that feminine nouns in the nominative cause adjectives to be lenited: *caileag bheag*, *cathair mhòr*, *madainn mhath*, *oidhche fhuar*, *uinneag fhosgailte*. This is still the case even when the nouns are definite: ***a' chaileag bheag***, ***a' mhadainn mhath***, etc.

Exercise 7B. Cuir Gàidhlig air:

1. The job is good.
2. Is the office open?
3. The school is closed.

Remember the difference between the two main jobs adjectives can do: they can describe the noun (attributive function) or they can finish the sense of the sentence (predicative function). Feminine nouns only cause adjectives to lenite when the adjectives are carrying out the attributive function: in other words, only when the adjective is PART OF the phrase along with the noun.

Examples:

a. Tha obair math.
   Work is good.

b. Tha obair mhath agam.
   I have a good job.

In Example (a), the adjective is NECESSARY for the meaning of the sentence. If you take the adjective away, the sentence does not make sense. Therefore, the adjective is the predicate of the sentence. So, even though it comes straight after the noun, it is NOT part of the noun phrase. In Example (b), you could take the adjective away and the sentence would still make sense (although it would tell you slightly less). In (b), the adjective is attributive (it is telling you more about the 'attributes' of the noun): therefore, it is part of the noun phrase and is lenited by the noun.

> You will learn more about using ***agam*** in Unit 11.

Exercise 7C. Cuir Beurla air:

1. A bheil an iris math?
2. Tha an t-sràid dùinte an-diugh.
3. Tha oifis mhòr agam.
4. Thuirt Iain gu bheil an fheòil math.

Exercise 7D. Cuir Gàidhlig air:

1. Iain said that the school is open.
2. Did Janet say that the office is cold?
3. They said that the bed is not bad.
4. Donald said that Calum said that the weather is good today.

Although 'feminine' (grammar) does not mean the same thing as 'feminine' or 'female' in other contexts, most female nouns are in fact feminine in Gaelic. Most nouns that end in *–ag* are also feminine (but not all). Another common ending for feminine nouns is *–ir*, but this ending does occur on several masculine nouns as well. Many body parts are feminine: ***sròn, sùil, amhaich, làmh, cas, òrdag, corrag***, etc. But there are also many masculine body parts.

Exercise 7E. Cuir an t-alt agus an t-ainmear ceart còmhla:

an, an, an, an, an, an, an, an, an (& lenition), an t-, ~~a' (& lenition)~~, a' (& lenition), a' (& lenition), a' (& lenition), a' (& lenition)

obair, aimsir, ~~Gàidhlig~~, Beurla, leabaidh, iris, oifis, sgoil, sràid, feòil, cathair, madainn, caileag, oidhche, uinneag

a' Ghàidhlig _____

_____

_____

Unit 7 Reading Texts:

Obair
An obair
A bheil obair agad?
Dè an obair a th' agad?

Obair mhath
Tha obair mhath agam

BUT
Tha an obair math

Aimsir mhath

BUT
Tha an aimsir math an-diugh

Ciamar a tha an aimsir?
Tha an aimsir math.

Leabaidh
Leabaidh mhòr
An leabaidh
An leabaidh mhòr

BUT
Tha an leabaidh mòr.

Iris
Iris bheag
An iris
An iris bheag

BUT
Tha an iris beag.

A bheil an iris math?
Tha, tha an iris math.

A bheil an iris bheag math?
Tha, tha an iris bheag math.

A bheil an iris bheag, mhath fosgailte?
Tha, tha an irish bheag, mhath fosgailte.

A bheil thu ag obair ann an oifis?
Tha.
An e oifis mhòr a th' ann?
Chan e; 's e oifis bheag a th' ann.

A bheil thu ag obair ann an oifis mhòr?
Tha, tha mi ag obair ann an oifis mhòr.

Tha an oifis air sràid mhòr.

Sgoil
An sgoil
Sgoil bheag
An sgoil bheag

BUT
Tha an sgoil beag.

An e sgoil mhath a th' ann?
'S e, 's e sgoil mhath a th' ann.

OR

A bheil an sgoil math?
Tha, tha an sgoil math.

Càit a bheil thu ag obair?
Tha mi ag obair ann an oifis bheag.
Càit a bheil an oifis?
Tha an oifis (bheag) ann an sgoil mhath.
Càit a bheil an sgoil?
Tha an sgoil (mhath) air sràid mhòr.
Càit a bheil an sgoil?
Tha an sgoil an seo ann an Obar Dheathain.

Summary of the feminine singular dative:

An adjective qualifying the noun will lenite if it begins with a lenitable consonant.	
The article will be:	... when the noun begins with:
a' (& lenition)	b, c, g, m, p
an t-	s (but not sg, sm, sp or st)
an (& lenition)	f
an	a, d, e, h, i, l, n, o, r, t, u

Unit 7 Dialogue:

Gòrdan is on the bus on his way to university, when he hears a woman talking with a Hebridean accent.

GÒRDAN: Madainn mhath. A bheil a' Ghàidhlig agaibh?
CATRÌONA: O, tha! Tha Gàidhlig gu leòr agam!
GÒRDAN: Cò às a tha sibh?
CATRÌONA: Tha mise à Barraigh. Cò às a tha sibh fhèin?
GÒRDAN: Tha mi à Sasainn.
CATRÌONA: B' àilleibh? An do dh'innis sibh dhomh gu bheil sibh à Sasainn?
GÒRDAN: Tha sin ceart. Thuirt mi gu bheil mi à Sasainn.
CATRÌONA: Ach ciamar a tha Gàidhlig agaibh fhèin?

GÒRDAN: Tha mi a' dèanamh Gàidhlig san oilthigh.
CATRÌONA: Càit? An seo ann an Obar Dheathain?
GÒRDAN: Tha sin ceart. Tha mi a' dèanamh Gàidhlig ann an Oilthigh Obar Dheathain.

Gàidhlig gu leòr: plenty of Gaelic [this is a common way of telling someone you are fluent]

UNIT 8: PAST TENSE OF 'TO BE'

Technical Terms Used in this Unit
No new technical terms are used in this Unit.

Faclan an Latha ... Your Daily Dose of Vocabulary

Verbs
a' tighinn — *coming*

Nouns
doras (m)	*door*	**an doras**	*the door*
baga (m)	*bag*	**am baga**	*the bag*
biadh (m)	*food*	**am biadh**	*the food*
aran (m)	*bread*	**an t-aran**	*the bread*
uisge (m)	*water*	**an t-uisge**	*the water*
gille* (m)	*boy*	**an gille**	*the boy*

Idioms
Tha ... ann — *... is there / ... exists / There is a ... / There are ...*

dhachaigh — *home – normally only used in this lenited form and normally used with movement, i.e. 'homewards'*

Adverbials
an-dè — *yesterday*
fad an latha — *all day*
aig an taigh — *at home*

*You already know another word for boy, **balach**. Both words are commonly used and known.

The past tense of **tha** is **bha**. It is used in exactly the same way as **tha** and means 'was' or 'were'.

Examples:

Bha mi sgìth an-dè.
I was tired yesterday.

Bha Mòrag ag obair fad an latha.
Morag was working all day.

Remember that the basic word order in Gaelic is Verb-Subject-Complement. Remember, also, that the subject of a sentence can be either a noun or a pronoun. Also remember that the personal pronouns are:

mi – I, me
thu – you (singular, informal)
e – he, him, it (masculine nouns)
i – she, her, it (feminine nouns)

sinn – we, us
sibh – you (polite or plural)
iad – they, them

Eacarsaich 8A. Cuir Gàidhlig air:

1. I was happy yesterday, but I am not happy today.
2. Mary was eating at home.
3. They were good.

The negative form is **cha robh**, which is used exactly like **chan eil**, and means 'was not' or 'were not'.

Examples:

Cha robh Iain aig an taigh an-dè.
Iain was not at home yesterday.

Cha robh sinn ag òl.
We were not drinking.

Eacarsaich 8B. Cuir Gàidhlig air:

1. The little girl was not tired.
2. The good book was not there.
3. The window was not open.

The question form is **an robh**, which is used exactly like **a bheil**, and means 'was ...?' or 'were ...?'

Examples:

An robh thu trang an-diugh?
Were you busy today?

An robh Tormod ag obair sa bhùth?
Was Norman working in the shop?

> This last example contains a dative, which you have not seen yet. The dative appears in unit 10.

Eacarsaich 8C. Cuir Gàidhlig air:

1. Was the happy boy at home all day yesterday?
2. Was the door shut today?
3. Were they tired or were they busy?

To make an indirect statement, you use the form **gun robh**, which works exactly like **gu bheil**, and means 'that ... was' or 'that ... were'.

Examples:

Chuala mi gun robh thu ag obair aig an taigh an-dè.
I heard that you were working at home yesterday.

Thuirt Dòmhnall gun robh an doras fosgailte.
Donald said that the door was open.

Eacarsaich 8D. Cuir Beurla air:

1. An tuirt Màiri gun robh i trang fad an latha an-dè?
2. Chuala mi gun robh sibh ag obair sa bhùth.
3. Cha tuirt thu gun robh thu aig an taigh an-diugh.

To make a negative indirect statement, you use the form **nach robh**, which works exactly like **nach eil**, and means 'that ... was not' or 'that ... were not'.

Examples:

Thuirt Seonag nach robh i a' tighinn dhachaigh.
Joan said that she was not coming home.

Chuala mi nach robh thu mòr.
I heard that you weren't big.

Eacarsaich 8E. Make three sentences using **nach robh**.

If you hear a question that begins with **an robh**, the 'yes' answer is **bha** and the 'no' answer is **cha robh**.

Unit 8 Reading Texts:

Bha Calum sgìth

Bha mi sgìth
Bha thu sgìth
Bha e sgìth
Bha i sgìth
Bha sinn sgìth

Bha sibh sgìth
Bha iad sgìth

Cha robh Calum sgìth
Cha robh mi sgìth
Cha robh thu sgìth
Cha robh e sgìth
Cha robh i sgìth
Cha robh sinn sgìth
Cha robh sibh sgìth
Cha robh iad sgìth

An robh Calum sgìth?
An robh mi sgìth?
An robh thu sgìth?
An robh e sgìth?
An robh i sgìth?
An robh sinn sgìth?
An robh sibh sgìth?
An robh iad sgìth?

An robh thu ag obair an-dè?
Bha.

An robh thu ag obair an-dè?
Cha robh.

An robh thu ag obair an-dè?
Bha, bha mi ag obair an-dè.

An robh thu ag obair an-dè?
Cha robh, cha robh mi ag obair an-dè.

Short Passage: Calum san Leabharlann (Calum in the Library)

Bha Calum trang ag obair san leabharlann an-dè. Chuala e Mairead a' tighinn tron doras. "Seadh, a Chaluim," thuirt i. "Ciamar a tha thu an-diugh?" "Tha mi trang agus sgìth," thuirt Calum, "ach tha mi toilichte gu leòr. Ciamar a tha thu fhèin?" "Chan eil dona," thuirt Mairead, "ach tha an cnatan orm." Bha Calum ag iarraidh ithe, ach cha robh biadh san leabharlann. "Bha mi ag obair fad an latha," thuirt e, "agus tha mi a' dol dhachaigh a-nis."

Leabharlann: library
Ag iarraidh: wanting

Summary of 'yes' and 'no' answers so far:

Question form:	'Yes' answer	'No' answer
A bheil … ?	**Tha**	**Chan eil**
An e … ?	**'S e**	**Chan e**
An tuirt … ?	**Thuirt / thubhairt**	**Cha tuirt / cha tubhairt**
An robh … ?	**Bha**	**Cha robh**

Unit 8 Dialogue:

Gòrdan joins the Gaelic class; he is one day late:

GÒRDAN:	Madainn mhath. Is mise Gòrdan.
NIALL:	Seadh, a dhuine. Is mise Niall. Dè do chor.
GÒRDAN:	Deagh chor, tapadh leat. Dè do chor fhèin?
NIALL:	Aidh, deagh chor.
MAIREAD:	Cha robh thu ann an-dè, an robh?
GÒRDAN:	Cha robh. Bha mi ag obair.
NIALL:	O, is ise Mairead.
GÒRDAN:	Hai, a Mhairead. Ciamar a tha thu?
MAIREAD:	Tha mi gu math. Cò às a tha thu, a Ghòrdan?
GÒRDAN:	Tha mi à Sasainn.
MAIREAD:	Ach tha thu a' dèanamh Gàidhlig san Oilthigh? Glè mhath!
GÒRDAN:	*looking over at the teacher, who is preparing the screen* An e sin an tidsear?
MAIREAD:	'S e.
GÒRDAN:	A bheil i math?
NIALL:	Tha. Tha i glè mhath.
GÒRDAN:	Tha mi duilich: dè thuirt thu?
NIALL:	Thuirt mi gu bheil i math.

MAIREAD: Thuirt thu gun robh thu ag obair an-dè. Càit an robh thu ag obair?
GÒRDAN: Aig an taigh. Bha mi ag obair aig an taigh fad an latha an-dè.

Duine: a person, a man

UNIT 9: PLURALS, POSSESSION AND IMPERATIVES

Technical Terms Used in this Unit

imperative   The part of the verb that is used for giving commands.

Faclan an Latha ... Your Daily Dose of Vocabulary

Nouns

rathad (m)	*road*	**an rathad**	*the road*
lagh (m/f)	*law*	**an lagh**	*the law*
cuspair (m)	*subject*	**an cuspair**	*the subject*
cànan* (m)	*language*	**an cànan**	*the language*
bràthair (m)	*brother*	**am bràthair**	*the brother*
cù (m)	*dog*	**an cù**	*the dog*

Conjunctions, Interrogatives and Prepositions

no	*or*	**ro**	*before*
dè?	*what?*	**fo**	*under*

*In some dialects, the noun ***cànain*** (note the slightly different spelling) is feminine.

There are several ways to make nouns plural in Gaelic. The simplest of all, and the most common, is to add the ending *–an* to the end of the word.

Examples:

caileagan
girls

uinneagan
windows

cànanan
languages

gillean
boys

Notice that this works for both masculine and feminine nouns.

Because of the broad-to-broad and slender-to-slender rule you already know, this ending has to be modified slightly if it is added to a noun that has a slender ending: -*ean*. The e lets the noun follow the slender-to-slender part of the rule.

Examples:

irisean
magazines

oifisean
offices

sràidean
streets

When the noun is in the nominative, the definite article (word for 'the') is **na**. This is the same for both masculine and feminine nouns.

Examples:

na caileagan
the girls

na cànanan
the languages

na sràidean
the streets

If the noun begins with a vowel, add h- immediately before the noun. This separates the two vowel sounds: Gaelic almost always tries to avoid having two vowel sounds coming together if there is any way to avoid it.

Examples:

na h-uinneagan
the windows

na h-irisean
the magazines

na h-oifisean
the offices

There are some variations on this theme, with slight differences. Some nouns add an extra sound in the middle of the word, with the ending becoming **–ichean** or **-aichean**. These are typically very short words in the first place, and often words that are borrowed from English.

Examples:

càraichean
cars

busaichean
buses

A few words double up the ending, resulting in an ending as *-annan* or *-eannan*. This is not very common.

Example:

oidhcheannan
nights

Some nouns form their plural by becoming slender: that is, an i is added before the final consonant or final group of consonants. These are almost always masculine nouns, and they are almost always fairly short words (normally either one or two syllables).

Example:

balaich
boys

This last group should be noted carefully. Keep a list of those nouns which form their nominative plural in this way (you could use a separate section in your notes or vocabulary book to start building up a list of these). It will sound very strange indeed to a Gaelic speaker's ears if you try to make one of these nouns plural by adding *-an*.

> **Other information:**
>
> The nouns that form their nominative plural by becoming slender also form their genitive singular in the same way. You will encounter the genitive later in the course.

The nouns we have so far that form their nominative plural by becoming slender are:

balach : **balaich**
bòrd : **bùird***
peann : **pinn**

*Notice that slenderising a word sometimes causes the vowel before the i to change as well. This kind of change also happens with the Gaelic word for a 'fish':

iasg : **èisg**

Other nouns you will encounter soon that form their plural like this:

oileanach : **oileanaich**
cat : **cait**
coineanach : **coineanaich**
radan : **radain**
ceann : **cinn**
bodach : **bodaich**

Many of these words have a nominative singular ending in either **–an** or **–ach**.

As always, if there are any words in these examples that you do not know yet, write them in your vocabulary book and look up their meaning in a dictionary or in your books.

Eacarsaich 9A. Make a list of all the nouns you have come across so far and write in their nominative plural form beside them.

From now on, the daily dose of vocabulary will show the way a noun forms its nominative plural.

Other information:

There are a few other ways in which some nouns form their nominative plural, but these are not common and can be learnt as you go along. There are some nouns that form their plural in irregular ways that simply have to be learnt as you encounter them.

In Gaelic, there is no verb 'to have'. If you want to say that you 'have' something, you must use one of two idioms. If you want to emphasise that you have something on a permanent basis (e.g. you 'own' it), you use the **preposition *le*** (which literally means 'with'). If you 'have' something in a more general way (including owning something), or temporarily (e.g. you have your book with you today), you use the preposition *aig* (which literally means 'at'). This second way of expressing possession is far more common than the first, and you will use it in the majority of your Gaelic conversations. You will come across the use of *le* later in the course.

Eisimpleirean:

Tha leabhar aig Màiri.
Mary has a book.

Tha peann aig Eilidh.
Helen has a pen.

Tha cù aig Ealasaid.
Elizabeth has a dog.

Eacarsaich 9B. Cuir Gàidhlig air:

1. Does Mary have a cat?
2. Helen does not have a car.
3. Elizabeth has pens.

Eacarsaich 9C. The students Iain, Ruaraidh, Sìne and Raonaid all have various items, as listed below. Answer the questions that follow, based on this list. When the questions become more complex, you will have to answer with a 'yes' or 'no' and also an explanation (in Gaelic).

Iain	peann	càr	iris
Ruaraidh	cù	leabhar	baga
Sìne	leabhar	cathair	peann
Raonaid	coineanach	iris	bòrd

1. A bheil càr aig Iain?
2. A bheil bòrd aig Sìne?
3. A bheil baga aig Raonaid?
4. A bheil iris aig Ruaraidh?
5. A bheil cù agus baga aig Ruaraidh?
6. A bheil cathair agus leabhar aig Sìne?
7. A bheil cù no cat aig Raonaid?
8. A bheil iris no leabhar aig Sìne?
9. Dè tha aig Ruaraidh?
10. Dè tha aig Sìne nach eil aig Iain?

Eacarsaich 9C Variation. For some speaking practice, you may prefer to try this exercise with a partner, either instead of writing the answers or after you have done so.

Possession

In order to express 'I have', 'you have', 'she has', etc., you must use the **prepositional pronouns** from the word ***aig***. These are:

agam (lit. 'at me')
agad (lit. 'at you')
aige (lit. 'at him')
aice (lit. 'at her')

againn (lit. 'at us')
agaibh (lit. 'at you' – plural)
aca (lit. 'at them')

Eisimpleirean:

Tha leabhar agam.
I have a book.

Chan eil peann agam.
I don't have a pen.

Tha obair mhath aice.
She has a good job.

Thuirt Dòmhnall nach eil cù aige.
Donald said that he doesn't have a dog.

Eacarsaich 9D. Work with the list of nouns that you made in 9A.

1. Write five sentences expressing 'I have' with single items (e.g. 'I have a cat').
2. Write five sentences expressing 'Do you have?' with single items.
3. Write five sentences expressing 'I don't have' with single items.
4. Write five sentences expressing 'I have' with plural items (e.g. 'I have magazines').

Other information:

Prepositional pronouns are another of the features of Celtic languages. *Agam* is simply *aig* plus *mi* squashed together to create a new word; *agad* is *aig* plus *tu*; *aige* is, more obviously, *aig* plus *e*, etc.

Giving Orders

To tell somebody to do something in Gaelic, you use the **imperative** form of the verb. With most verbs, the **imperative** is a bit shorter than the verbal noun, and it often has a slender ending. Unfortunately, this is only a rough guide. There is no substitute for learning *both* forms for each verb.

Eisimpleirean:

a' fuireach
staying / living

fuirich!
stay!

ag òl
drinking

òl!
drink!

ag ithe
eating

ith!
eat!

There is also a plural form of the **imperative**, which we will see in a later unit.

Other information:

The **imperative** is also known as the root of the verb, and you will see why later.

Unit 9 Reading Texts:

Na Caileagan... agus Na Balaich

Tha trì caileagan a' tighinn bhon t-sràid tro dhoras an leabharlainn. Is iad Mairead, Màiri agus Sorcha. Tha bagaichean aig Mairead agus Sorcha, ach chan eil baga aig Màiri. Tha leabhraichean aig Màiri, agus tha peann aice. Tha am baga aig Mairead fosgailte. Tha e falamh. Chan eil leabhraichean no pinn aig Mairead. Tha am baga aig Sorcha dùinte, ach tha e làn. Tha gu leòr leabhraichean agus pinn aice.

***

Tha trì balaich a' tighinn bhon t-sràid tro dhoras an taigh-seinnse. Is iad Niall, Calum agus Gòrdan. Chan eil bagaichean no leabhraichean no pinn aca. Tha Niall ag ràdh gu bheil e a' dol don taigh-beag. Tha Calum ag ràdh gu bheil e ag iarraidh pinnt, ach tha Gòrdan ag ràdh nach eil airgead aige.

Taigh-seinnse: pub
Taigh-beag: toilet
Airgead: money

Summary

1. Nouns form plurals by adding *-(e)an*, *-(a)ichean*, *-(e)annan* or by slenderising: *-i-*.

2. You express possession with the preposition *aig*.

3. When it is a pronoun and not a noun that is doing the possessing, you need to use *agam*, *agad*, *aige*, *aice*, *againn*, *agaibh*, *aca*.

Unit 9 Dialogue:

NIALL: Dè do chor, a Chaluim? A bheil thu ag iarraidh dol don taigh-seinnse?
CALUM: Tha: tha am pathadh orm. Càit a bheil Gòrdan?
NIALL: Chan eil fhios a'm. A bheil e aig an taigh?
CALUM: Chan eil.

Calum phones Gòrdan
GÒRDAN: Hai. Gòrdan an seo.
CALUM: Feasgar math, a Ghòrdan. Tha mi fhèin agus Niall a' dol don taigh-seinnse. A bheil am pathadh ort?
GÒRDAN: O, tha!
CALUM: A bheil thu fhèin a' tighinn, mathà?
GÒRDAN: Tha. Tapadh leat. Dè an taigh-seinnse?

Calum asks Niall the same question then gets back to the phone
CALUM: Tha sinn a' dol don Mhachar.
GÒRDAN: Glè mhath. Tioraidh an-dràsta, mathà.
CALUM: Tioraidh.

The three of them meet outside the pub
NIALL: A bheil sinn a' dol a-steach, mathà?
GÒRDAN: Tha.

They go in and find a place at the bar
NIALL: Tha mise a' dol don taigh-beag.
CALUM: Seadh. Tha am pathadh orm. Tha mi ag iarraidh pinnt.

Gòrdan looks in his wallet and realises he has not brought any cash to the pub
GÒRDAN: Tha mi duilich, a dhuine. Chan eil airgead agam.
CALUM: Obh obh!

mathà: then [not used to denote time; this 'then' only means 'therefore']

UNIT 10: MASCULINE DATIVE

Technical Terms Used in this Unit
There are no new technical terms in this Unit.

Faclan an Latha ... Your Daily Dose of Vocabulary

Verbs

a' tighinn	*coming*
a' dol	*going*
a' fuireach	*staying*
a' falbh	*going (away)*

Nouns

gàrradh (m)	*garden*	**an gàrradh**	*the garden*
gàrraidhean	*gardens*	**anns a' ghàrradh**	*in the garden*
fear (m)	*man*	**am fear**	*the man*
fir	*men*	**aig an fhear**	*at the man (e.g. belonging to the man)*
boireannach (m)	*woman*	**am boireannach**	*the woman*
boireannaich	*women*	**aig a' bhoireannach**	*at the woman*

Adjectives

brèagha	*beautiful*
grannda	*ugly*
luath	*fast*
slaodach	*slow*
blàth	*warm*
fuar	*cold*

Prepositions

ann an	*in*	**anns a'** **anns an** **anns an t-**	*in the*
do	*to*	**don** **don t-**	*to the*
bho	*from*	**bhon** **bhon t-**	*from the*
air	*on*	**air a'** **air an** **air an t-**	*on the*

In Unit 6, you learned how to use the masculine nominative singular. In this Unit, you will learn how masculine nouns work in the dative singular.

In the context of Gaelic, the word 'dative' simply means 'the way a noun behaves after most prepositions.' In modern Gaelic, the dative is only used when the noun is definite (i.e. when there is a word for 'the' before the noun).

Recall how masculine nouns work with the definite article and adjectives in the nominative:

am   when the noun begins with b, f, m or p
an t- when the noun begins with a vowel
an   when the noun begins with any other letter
Adjectives do not lenite.

Eisimpleirean:

am balach math
the good boy

an càr luath
the fast car

Tha taigh brèagha aig Iain.
Iain has a beautiful house.

When a simple preposition comes before a definite masculine noun, it can cause changes in (1) the article, (2) the noun and (3) the adjective (if there is one).

The following prepositions cause these changes (and so we say that they 'take the dative'):

do
bho
ann an
air
aig

Bringing the prepositions and definite articles together also causes some of the prepositions to change. For example, the prepositions that end in *–o* merge with the article:

do : don
bho : bhon

Some of the prepositions gain an *–s* ending: so, **ann an** becomes **anns**, losing the second word altogether. However, neither **aig** nor **air** change at all.

The basic pattern for the masculine dative singular is as follows:

a' when the noun begins with b, c, g, m or p. **The noun lenites**.
an when the noun begins with f. **The noun lenites**.
an t- when the noun begins with sa, se, si, so, su, sl, sn, sr.
an when the noun begins with any other letter
An adjective that follows the noun will lenite if possible.

> Does this pattern remind you of anything you have already learnt?

Eisimpleirean:

an doras	an t-uisge	am bòrd
the door	*the water*	*the table*
an doras mòr	an t-uisge blàth	am bòrd beag
the big door	*the warm water*	*the little table*
aig an doras	anns an uisge	air a' bhòrd
at the door	*in the water*	*on the table*
aig an doras mhòr	anns an uisge bhlàth	air a' bhòrd bheag
at the big door	*in the warm water*	*on the little table*

> Tip: you may find it useful to recite this table or even to learn it off by heart if you have the time. Many people find it easier to remember patterns by learning examples off by heart than by learning the pattern academically.

With the prepositions that merge with the article, two things can happen, depending on the preference of the person who is writing or speaking: either the article is absorbed into the new word or else the article is repeated.

Eisimpleirean:

bhon bhalach
from the boy

OR

bhon a' bhalach
from the boy

Both possibilities are equally valid. The former is more common in writing, so that is what is favoured in this textbook, but you should be able to recognise the other version, too.

Eacarsaich 10A. Cuir Beurla air:

1. Bha an duine grannda ag obair aig a' bhòrd bheag.
2. A bheil Sìne a' tighinn bhon Eilean Sgiathanach* an-diugh?
3. Cha robh Màrtainn a' dol don ghàrradh, an robh?
4. Tha mi a' fuireach aig an taigh an-diugh.

*An t-Eilean Sgiathanach = (the island of) Skye

Eacarsaich 10B. Cuir Gàidhlig air:

1. in the garden
2. at the door
3. on the road
4. to the big garden

5. from the little door
6. on the cold table

Eacarsaich 10C. Dè a' Bheurla a tha air:

1. Bha càr beag grannda aig a' bhoireannach an-dè, ach chuala mi gu bheil i anns a' chàr mhòr bhrèagha an-diugh.
2. Thuirt Dòmhnall gu bheil e a' fuireach anns a' chàr an-dràsta.
3. An robh pinn aca air a' bhòrd, no an robh pinn aca aig an taigh?

The prepositions that take the dative

do *to*
de *of, off*
bho *from*
o *from*
a *to*
à *from, out of*
le *with*
ri *to*
mu *about*
fo *under*
ro *before*
tro *through*
gu *to*
air *on*
aig *by, at*
ann an *in*

Eacarsaich 10D. Work with two partners (Obraichibh còmhla ri dithis eile).

1. Refer to a list of all the masculine nouns you currently know.
2. The first person says the noun on its own (e.g. 'balach').
3. The second person says the noun with its nominative article (e.g. 'am balach').
4. The third person says the noun with an adjective (e.g. 'balach math').
5. The first person says the noun with article and adjective (e.g. 'am balach math').

6. The second person says a preposition with the noun and article (e.g. 'don bhalach').
7. The third person says preposition, article, noun and adjective (e.g. 'don bhalach mhath').
8. Repeat until told to stop, with each person in the group having a turn at picking a noun. Even if you exhaust your supply of nouns, go back to the start and keep going. Try to help each other if you get stuck, but only help if you are sure. If you are unsure, make a note of the noun that you were stuck on, move on to another one, and ask for help when you get the chance.

Unit 10 Reading Texts:

Different examples of how to tackle exercise 10D

IAIN:	balach
MÀIRI:	am balach
SORCHA:	balach math
IAIN:	am balach math
MÀIRI:	don bhalach
SORCHA:	don bhalach mhath
IAIN:	fear
MÀIRI:	am fear
SORCHA:	fear mòr
IAIN:	am fear mòr
MÀIRI:	aig an fhear
SORCHA:	aig an fhear mhòr
IAIN:	boireannach
MÀIRI:	am boireannach
SORCHA:	boireannach brèagha
IAIN:	am boireannach brèagha
MÀIRI:	bhon bhoireannach
SORCHA:	bhon bhoireannach bhrèagha
IAIN:	peann
MÀIRI:	am peann
SORCHA:	peann beag
IAIN:	am peann beag
MÀIRI:	air a' pheann
SORCHA:	air a' pheann bheag

Short Passages

Bha Sorcha ag iarraidh peann. Thuirt Mairead gun robh peann air a' bhòrd. Ach cha robh: bha am peann air a' chathair.

Bha an t-acras air Calum. Bha e ag iarraidh biadh. Cha robh biadh aige. An robh biadh anns a' chidsin? Cha robh.

Bha am pathadh air Màiri. Bha i ag iarraidh uisge. Bha uisge aice aig an taigh.

Bha Dòmhnall ag iarraidh tighinn a-steach. Bha e a' gnogadh air an doras, ach cha robh Iain ann.

Bha boireannach ag obair anns a' ghàrradh bhlàth fad an latha. Bha an t-acras oirre: bha i ag iarraidh aran ithe.

Cidsin: kitchen
A' gnogadh: knocking

Summary

1. The dative case is used only when a noun is definite.
2. The dative occurs when a simple preposition comes before a definite noun.
3. The dative can change the preposition, the article, the noun and the adjective.

The article will be:	... when the noun begins with:
a' (& lenition)	b, c, g, m, p
an t-	s (but not sg, sm, sp or st)
an (& lenition)	f
an	a, d, e, h, i, l, n, o, r, t, u

Any adjective following the noun will lenite if possible.

UNIT 11: FEMININE DATIVE

Technical Terms Used in this Unit
There are no new technical terms in this Unit.

Faclan an Latha ... Your Daily Dose of Vocabulary

Verbs

chunnaic	*saw*
am faca?	*did ... see?*
chan fhaca	*did not see*
a' smèideadh (air)	*waving to/at*

Nouns

eaglais (f)	*church*	**an eaglais**	*the church*
eaglaisean	*churches*	**anns an eaglais**	*in the church*
sgeulachd (f)	*story*	**an sgeulachd**	*the story*
sgeulachdan	*stories*	**anns an sgeulachd**	*in the story*

Adverbs

tric	*often*

Prepositions

le	*with*	**leis a'**	*with the*
		leis an	
		leis an t-	
fo	*under*	**fon**	*under the*
		fon t-	
mu	*about*	**mun**	*about the*
		mun t-	
tro	*through*	**tron**	*through the*
		tron t-	

The dative also affects feminine nouns. However, with feminine nouns, the definite article and the first letter of the noun do not change. Similarly, if the adjective was able to lenite in the nominative, it still lenites in the dative. With feminine nouns, the change for the dative is an internal one.

When a feminine noun is in the dative, the ending of the noun becomes slender. This change will only take place if the ending of the noun allows it. It will happen only if the noun ends in a broad consonant (or cluster of broad consonants). If the noun is already slender, it cannot become more slender. If the noun ends in a vowel, it does not change.

Similarly, an adjective following the noun will also become slender if possible. Again, this only happens if the adjective's ending allows it. The adjective will change only if it ends in a broad consonant or cluster of broad consonants.

Reminder of the articles and the first letters of feminine nouns:

The article will be:	... when the noun begins with:
a' (**& lenition**)	b, c, g, m, p
an t-	s (but not <u>sg</u>, <u>sm</u>, <u>sp</u> or <u>st</u>)
an (**& lenition**)	f
an	a, d, e, h, i, l, n, o, r, t, u

Here are some of the feminine nouns you know:

caileag
cathair
eaglais
feòil
iris
leabaidh
madainn
oidhche
oifis
sgoil
sràid
uinneag

> Out of this list of common feminine nouns, how many of them will actually change in the dative?

Eacarsaich 11A. Cuir Gàidhlig air:

1. The ugly girl.
2. The ugly chair.
3. The ugly church.
4. The beautiful meat.
5. The beautiful magazine.
6. The beautiful bed.
7. The cold morning.
8. The cold night.
9. The cold office.
10. The warm school.
11. The warm street.
12. The warm window.

When a simple preposition meets a definite feminine noun, the noun is slenderised, as in the example:

a' chaileag : don chaileig

Any adjective that is qualifying the noun will also slenderise if possible:

a' chaileag mhòr : don chaileig mhòir

Eisimpleirean:

a' mhadainn bhrèagha
the beautiful morning

anns a' mhadainn bhrèagha
in the beautiful morning

an sgoil mhath
the good school

aig an sgoil mhaith
at the good school

a' chaileag bheag
the little girl

aig a' chaileig bhig
at the little girl

Notice that **beag** becomes **big** when it slenderises (and turns into a visual false friend), and so the lenited form **bheag** becomes **bhig**. This kind of thing happens to a small number of very short adjectives.

Nouns that end in *-achd* never slenderise. All nouns with that ending are feminine, but do not change for the dative:

anns an sgeulachd mhaith
in the good story

Eacarsaich 11B. Cuir Beurla air:

1. Chunnaic mi gun robh Eilidh a' smèideadh orm tron uinneig.
2. Bha sgeulachd mhath anns an iris bhig.
3. An robh sibh tric ag obair anns an sgoil mhòir?

Other Information:

Some older speakers do still use the dative even with indefinite feminine nouns. Some educated speakers also do this, and it is common for people to do it when they are using formal or technical language. You may see indefinite feminine datives in older texts or in formal or technical writing. The main feature of an indefinite feminine dative would be the slenderisation: *aig uinneig* (at a window)

Eacarsaich 11C. Put appropriate feminine nouns after these articles:

1. leis an...............
2. anns a'..............
3. air an t-.............
4. aig a'...............
5. tron.................

Eacarsaich 11D. Obraichibh còmhla ri dithis eile.

1. Refer to a list of all the feminine nouns you currently know.
2. The first person says the noun on its own (e.g. 'uinneag').
3. The second person says the noun with its nominative article (e.g. 'an uinneag').
4. The third person says the noun with an adjective (e.g. 'uinneag mhath').
5. The first person says the noun with article and adjective (e.g. 'an uinneag mhath').
6. The second person says a preposition with the noun and article (e.g. 'don uinneig').
7. The third person says preposition, article, noun and adjective (e.g. 'don uinneig mhaith').
8. Repeat until told to stop, with each person in the group having a turn at picking a noun. Even if you exhaust your supply of nouns, go back to the start and keep going. Try to help each other if you get stuck, but only help if you are sure. If you are unsure, make a note of the noun that you were stuck on, move on to another one, and ask for help when you get the chance.

More on Expressing Possession

In Unit 9, you learned how to say 'to have' by using the preposition *aig*. You also learned that you must use the compound forms in order to express 'I have', 'you have', etc.:

agam
agad
aige
aice

againn
agaibh
aca

You also use these forms of *aig* to express 'my', 'your', 'his', 'her', etc.:

an càr agam [lit. 'the car at me']
my car

an leabhar aige
his book

a' chathair aice
her chair

an oifis agad
your office

This also works if you use people's names instead of the prepositional pronouns:

am peann aig Iain
Iain's pen

an taigh aig Mairead
Margaret's house

an sgoil aig Ruaraidh
Rory's school

However, there is a more common way of expressing this kind of possession when using people's names. There is also another way of saying 'my', 'your', etc. You will see this in a later unit.

Unit 11 Reading Texts:
Tha fear ag innse sgeulachd bheag mu eaglais:

"Bha eaglais bheag anns a' bhaile mhòr. Bha fir agus boireannaich a' dol don eaglais anns a' mhadainn, agus bha balaich agus caileagan a' dol ann anns an fheasgar. Cha robh duine a' dol ann air an oidhche."

Duine: man, a man/ person, a person [but also means, as here, 'anyone']

Oidhche: night [notice that Gaelic says 'on the night' for 'at night']

An Latha Agam – My Day

Bha mise ag obair anns an oifis bhig anns a' mhadainn an-dè. Cha robh duine ann ach mi fhèin. Bha mi glè thrang agus cha robh mi toilichte. Bha an t-acras orm, ach cha robh biadh anns a' bhaga agam. Chunnaic mi gun robh doras a' chidsin fosgailte. Anns a' chidsin, chunnaic mi aran, ach cha robh mi ag iarraidh aran: bha mi ag iarraidh cèic! Chan fhaca mi càil ann. Bha bùth air an t-sràid. Bha mi ag iarraidh dol don bhùth, ach bha an t-uisge ann: bha e fliuch agus fuar, agus cha toil leam sin!

Bùth: shop

Summary

1. The dative case is used only when a noun is definite in modern Gaelic.
2. The dative occurs when a simple preposition comes before a definite noun.
3. The dative can change the preposition, the article, the noun and the adjective.

The article will be:	... when the noun begins with:
a' (& lenition)	b, c, g, m, p
an t-	s (but not <u>sg</u>, <u>sm</u>, <u>sp</u> or <u>st</u>)
an (& lenition)	f
an	a, d, e, h, i, l, n, o, r, t, u

Any adjective following the noun will lenite if possible.
Both the noun and the adjective will slenderise if possible.

Unit 11 Dialogue:

SEONAIDH: Dè tha sin?
MÀIRI: 'S e iris a th' ann.
SEONAIDH: Chunnaic mi sin! Ach *dè* an iris a th' ann?
MÀIRI: 'S e *Der Spiegel* a th' ann.
SEONAIDH: O, cò às a tha sin? An e iris Ghearmailteach a th' ann?
MÀIRI: 'S e; tha sin ceart. 'S e iris Ghearmailteach a th' ann. Tha mi a' dèanamh

	Gearmailtis anns an Oilthigh.
SEONAIDH:	Cha robh fhios a'm gun robh thu a' dèanamh sin. 'S e cuspair math a tha sin.
MÀIRI:	'S e. Is toil leam cànanan. An toil leat fhèin cànanan?
SEONAIDH:	Chan eil mi math air cànanan, ach is toil leam Gàidhlig.

Gearmailteach: German
Gearmailtis: German (language)

UNIT 12: PAST TENSE

Technical Terms Used in this Unit

Pre-verb(al) A pre-verb is a little word or prefix that is attached to the beginning of a verb, or that sits in front of a verb. It usually modifies the meaning or the tense, etc. Sometimes we call these pre-verbal particles.

root The most basic form of a verb. The root is often shorter than the verbal noun. With many verbs, the root has a slender ending. It is exactly the same as the imperative singular. When we call it the root, we are referring to the fact that it is the part of the verb that forms the basis for making the tenses.

Faclan an Latha ... Your Daily Dose of Vocabulary

Adverbs

fad an latha	*all day*	***fhathast**	*yet*
fada	*long*		

Nouns

litir (f)	*letter*	**an litir**	*the letter*
litrichean	*letters*	**anns an litir**	*in the letter*

Adjectives

air fad (follows the noun) — *all*

* Note that the *fh* is pronounced [h] in this word.

In the early stages in Gaelic, you can get by talking about things that happened in the past tense by using **bha** and the verbal nouns, just as you use **tha** and verbal nouns when talking about the present tense. Soon, though, you will start to hear people using the simple past tense, or you will want to express yourself more accurately or more precisely. In this unit, we begin using the simple past tense of regular verbs.

There are two main groups of verbs in Gaelic: regular and irregular verbs. Regular verbs are ones that follow predictable patterns: in other words, if you know the pattern, you can predict how the past, future, etc. will work, even if you have never seen that verb before. Irregular verbs do not follow predictable patterns, so each part of an irregular verb has to be learnt from scratch as new vocabulary. The good news is that almost all verbs in Gaelic are regular. In fact, there are only ten irregular verbs, as well as the two auxiliary verbs, *is* and *tha*, and there are a small number of others that exist only in partial form.

The past tense in Gaelic consists of two main forms, which we call **independent** and **dependent**. As you might guess from the name, the **independent** form of the verb can stand alone, without any other words or **pre-verbal** particles supporting it. The **dependent** form must always appear with another word. We have already seen this happening with the verbs we know.

Here is a reminder of the verbs we already know (none of these are regular), this time with their **independent** and **dependent** forms marked:

Dependent form:	Independent form:
A bheil ... ? **Chan eil** **Gu bheil** **Nach eil**	Tha
An e ... ? **Chan e** **Gur e** **Nach e**	'S e
An tuirt ... ? **Cha tuirt** **Gun tuirt** **Nach tuirt**	Thuirt / thubhairt
An robh ... ?	Bha

Cha <u>robh</u> Gun <u>robh</u> Nach <u>robh</u>	
Am <u>faca</u>...? Chan <u>fhaca</u> Gum <u>faca</u> Nach <u>fhaca</u>	Chunnaic
An <u>cuala</u>...? Cha <u>chuala</u> Gun <u>cuala</u> Nach <u>cuala</u>	Chuala

As you can see, the **independent** form is the part of the verb that we use to make a positive statement or a 'yes' answer. The **dependent** form is the part that appears in the simple questions or 'no' answers. It is important to understand and remember this before you go on and learn how to make the tenses.

Here is a reminder of other verbal nouns you already know. As always, if you do not know what they mean, look them up.

dol
falbh
fuireach
ithe
obair
òl
tighinn

Two of these, ***dol*** and ***tighinn***, are irregular verbs and will be dealt with later.

Here are some additional verbs from elsewhere in the course:

bruidhinn
ceannachd
cluich
coimhead
danns
dràibheadh

èisteachd
freagairt
gabhail
leughadh
peantadh
reic
seinn
sgioblachadh
sgrìobhadh
siubhal
smaoineachadh
snàmh
tachairt
togail

As you know, when you use these verbal nouns in a sentence with **tha**, you would add the **pre-verb** a' or ag to show that you are using the '-ing' form of the verb. E.g.:

Tha mi a' leughadh

I am reading

Bha mi ag èisteachd

I was listening

When do you use a' rather than ag?

To make the past tense, you need to find the **root** of the verb. The **root** is always exactly the same as the imperative, which you learned in Unit 9. Here are the verbal nouns again, along with their roots:

bruidhinn   -   bruidhinn
ceannachd   -   ceannaich

cluich	-	cluich
coimhead	-	coimhead
danns	-	danns
dràibheadh	-	dràibh
èisteachd	-	èist
*falbh	-	falbh
freagairt	-	freagair
fuireach	-	fuirich
gabhail	-	gabh
ithe	-	ith
leughadh	-	leugh
obair	-	obair
òl	-	òl
peantadh	-	peant
reic	-	reic
seinn	-	seinn
sgioblachadh	-	sgioblaich
sgrìobhadh	-	sgrìobh
siubhal	-	siubhail
smaoineachadh	-	smaoinich
snàmh	-	snàmh
tachairt	-	tachair
togail	-	tog

> *Although the **root** of ***falbh*** is ***falbh***, the verb is in such common use that a peculiarity has developed. The imperative was ***fhalbh***, but with a /h/ sound at the beginning. Probably because of the way Gaelic spelling works, this has changed the word, so that the imperative is now written ***thalla***.

To make the past tense:
1. Find the **root**;
2. Lenite the **root** if possible.

This gives you the **independent** form of the past tense.

Eisimpleirean:

bruidhinn!
speak!

bhruidhinn
spoke

danns!
dance!

dhanns
danced

gabh!
take!

ghabh
took

To make a sentence, add a subject after the verb, and any other elements as necessary:

Bhruidhinn mi.
I spoke.

Bhruidhinn Iain ri Mòrag an-dè.
Iain spoke to Morag yesterday.

Ghabh e grèim air an làimh.
He took hold of the handle.

(2b.) This works for all of the lenitable consonants, but, as we know, the vowels and some consonants do not lenite. If a consonant does not lenite, the **independent** form of the past tense is exactly the same as the **root**:

smaoinich!
think!

smaoinich
thought

reic!
sell!

reic
sold

(2c.) If the word begins with a vowel, add **dh'** to the start of the word (with no space between the apostrophe and the rest of the word):

òl!
drink!

dh'òl
drank

ith!
eat!

dh'ith
ate

(2d.) When the letter *f* is lenited, the resulting combination is silent. So, if the word starts with *f*, look for the second letter. If the second letter is a vowel, then the lenited word sounds like it starts with a vowel; if the second letter is a consonant, then the lenited word sounds like it starts with that consonant. To make the past tense of a word that begins with *f*, lenite the *f* and then treat the rest of the word as before:

fuirich!
stay!

dh'fhuirich
stayed

freagair!
answer!

fhreagair
answered

Words beginning with *f* behave in two different ways, then, depending on the second letter in the word. Be careful of this.

3. Add the small word ***do*** before the **root** to create the **dependent** form of the verb. Then add the question word or negative marker or whatever other part you need:

an do bhruidhinn?
did ... speak?

cha do bhruidhinn
... did not speak

gun do bhruidhinn
that ... spoke

an do sgrìobh?
did ... write?

cha do sgrìobh
... did not write

nach do sgrìobh
that ... did not write

an do dh'obair?
did ... work?

cha do dh'obair
... did not work

nach do dh'obair
that ... did not work

As always, the phrase that contains the verb comes first in the sentence, followed by the subject, followed by the rest of the sentence.

Eisimpleirean:

Dh'fhuirich mi aig an taigh fad an latha an-diugh.
I stayed at home all day today.

An do dh'fhuirich thu fada?
Did you stay long?

Eacarsaich 12A. Fill in the blanks (Lìonaibh na beàrnan):

1. An do _____ thu litir an-dè? [READ or WRITE – you choose]
2. _____ [answer 'no']
3. Thuirt Mìchel gun do _____ e uisge anns a' mhadainn an-diugh, ach chan eil mi a' smaoineachadh gun do _____. [DRINK]
4. Cha do _____ thu am baga. [PICK UP]
5. An cuala tu gun do _____ Mairead ri Seonag an-dè? [SPEAK]

In the past tense, the question words *dè*, *cò*, *ciamar*, *cuin*, and *carson* all take the **independent** form of the verb:

Dè dh'òl thu?
What did you drink?

Cuin a dh'fhalbh thu?
When did you go away?

Carson a cheannaich thu an càr?
Why did you buy the car?

As usual, the word for 'yes' is the same as the form that you use to make a positive statement – i.e. the **independent** form of the verb. The word for 'no' is the same as the form you use to make a negative statement – i.e. the **dependent** form.

Eisimpleirean:

An do pheant thu an taigh fhathast?
Did you paint the house yet?

Cha do pheant – bha mi ro thrang.
No – I was too busy.

An do dh'òl thu an t-uisge-beatha air fad?
Did you drink all the whisky?

Dh'òl.
Yes.

Eacarsaich 12B. Sgrìobh seantansan.

1. Pick five verbs beginning with at least three of the different kinds of letters (e.g. lenitable consonant, unlenitable consonant, vowel, *f* +consonant, *f*+vowel).
2. Write a positive statement in the past tense using each verb.
3. Write a negative statement in the past tense using each verb.
4. Write a question in the past tense using each verb, and give the 'yes' or 'no' answer.

Unit 12 Reading Texts:

Bhruidhinn an tidsear fad an latha, agus bha i glè sgìth!
An do bhruidhinn thu ri Calum a-raoir?
Cò bhruidhinn?
Cha do bhruidhinn mi fhathast.

Cheannaich mi peann math anns a' bhùth.
An do cheannaich Iain deoch-làidir an-dè?
Cò cheannaich an taigh?
Dè cheannaich thu anns a' bhùth?
Cha do cheannaich mi an iris sin fhathast.

Dh'èist mi ris an rèidio anns a' mhadainn. Bha e math: is toil leam an rèidio. Cha do dh'èist mi ri càil an-dè: bha mi glè thrang ag obair.

Leugh Seonaidh an leabhar Gàidhlig aige. Cha do leugh e an leabhar Lagh aige. Cha toil leis Lagh.

Dè leugh thu an-dè?
Leugh mi iris.

An Latha aig Catrìona – Catriona's Day

Choimhead Catrìona tron uinneig don bhùth. Bha irisean, leabhraichean agus pinn ann. Bha Catrìona ag iarraidh leughadh. Anns a' bhùth, cheannaich Catrìona iris mhath. Leugh i an iris anns a' mhadainn. Chluich i an giotàr aice anns an fheasgar. Dh'èist i ris an rèidio agus sheinn i fhèin. Smaoinich i gun do sheinn i glè mhath.

Summary

1. Make the **independent** form:

	Find the root			
	lenite the root if possible	add **dh'** to vowels	lenite *f*	add **dh'** to *f* if it is followed by a vowel
Root	coimhead	obair!	freagair!	fosgail!
Past tense	choimhead	dh'obair	fhreagair	dh'fhosgail
Root	sgrìobh!			
Past tense	sgrìobh			

2. Make the **dependent** form:

Add ***do*** to make **dependent** form			
Choimhead	Dh'obair	Fhreagair	Dh'fhosgail
An do choimhead?	An do dh'obair?	An do fhreagair?	An do dh'fhosgail?
Sgrìobh			
An do sgrìobh?			

Unit 12 Dialogue:

NIALL: Am faca tu an tidsear an-dè?
CALUM: Chunnaic.
NIALL: An do bhruidhinn thu rithe mun leabhar?
CALUM: Cha do bhruidhinn. Dè thuirt i?
NIALL: Thuirt i gun robh i a' smaoineachadh gun do cheannaich thu an leabhar ceàrr.
CALUM: Obh obh! Cha robh fhios a'm!
NIALL: Cò reic an leabhar dhut?
CALUM: Reic a' bhùth.
NIALL: An do leugh thu fhathast e?
CALUM: Cha do leugh. An do leugh thu fhèin an leabhar ceart fhathast?
NIALL: Cha do leugh.
CALUM: An do leugh Mairead e?
NIALL: Leugh. Thuirt i gun robh e math.
CALUM: Tha mi duilich nach eil e agam, mathà!

ceàrr: wrong

UNIT 13: EMPHATIC PRONOUNS AND PREPOSITIONAL PRONOUNS

Technical Terms Used in this Unit

suffix
: An ending that can be added to a word to change or emphasise its meaning.

paradigm
: The list of forms that a word can take when it includes the sense of the pronouns. In Gaelic, the paradigm is usually seven forms, e.g.: *I, you, he, she, we, you, they*

Faclan an Latha – Your Daily Dose of Vocabulary

Adjectives etc.

air bhioran	*excited*	**deiseil**	*ready, finished*

Nouns

uisge-beatha (m)	*whisky*	**an t-uisge-beatha**	*the whisky*
cèilidh (f)	*ceilidh (social gathering)*	**a' chèilidh**	*the ceilidh*
cèilidhean	*ceilidhs*	**aig a' chèilidh**	*at the ceilidh*

Adverbs, conjunctions, etc.

a-raoir	*last night*	**oir**	*because*
idir	*at all*	**a-mach**	*out, outside (with movement)*
... air fad	*all the ...*	**a-steach**	*in, inside (with movement)*

Verbs

a' dèanamh	*doing, making*	**cha d' rinn**	*... did not do/make*
rinn	*did, made*	**gun d' rinn**	*that ... did/made*
an d' rinn?	*did ... do/make?*	**nach d' rinn**	*that ... did not do/make*

You know that the personal pronouns are:

mi   *I, me*
thu *you* (singular, informal)
e   *he, him* (also *it*)
i   *she, her* (also *it*)

sinn *we, us*
sibh *you* (plural or polite)
iad *they, them*

In English, when you want to emphasise these pronouns, you can do so by putting stress on the words with your voice: we sometimes show this in writing by underlining, using italics or using bold print. In Gaelic, there is a set of **suffixes** which we add to the pronouns in order to emphasise them. You have already encountered some of them. The complete set of emphatic pronouns is:

mise   *I, me*
thusa   *you* (singular, informal)
esan   *he, him, it*
ise *she, her, it*

sinne   *we, us*
sibhse *you* (plural or polite)
iadsan *they, them*

Which ones did you already know?

Remember the endings of these emphatic pronouns, as they are also used to emphasise other classes of words, such as nouns. Here are the endings on their own:

-se (-sa, when it comes after a word other than ***mi***)
-sa
-san
-se

-(n)e
-se
-san

Eacarsaich 13A. Cuir Gàidhlig air (and notice the words that are stressed):

1. <u>I</u> didn't write a letter today; did <u>you</u>?
2. Did <u>you</u> dance yesterday?
3. I heard that <u>she</u> drank all the whisky.
4. Iain bought a car, but <u>we</u> didn't drive it.

Eacarsaich 13B. Cuir Beurla air (use an underline to emphasise the words that are stressed):

1. Is mise Marsaili; dè an t-ainm a th' ortsa?
2. Sheinn esan aig a' chèilidh a-raoir, ach cha do sheinn ise.
3. Chunnaic mi film math a-raoir, ach chan fhaca sibhse e.

Eacarsaich 13C. Lìon na beàrnan:

ise   *ise*   *esan*   *esan*

Chunnaic mi Iain an-dè. Bha e trang. Thuirt e gun robh Marsaili sa bhùth, ach cha robh trang idir. Thuirt Iain gun robh _____ sgìth, ach thuirt Marsaili nach robh _____ sgìth, oir cha robh i ag obair an-diugh. Bha an uinneag mhòr fosgailte sa bhùth, agus thuirt Marsaili gun robh i fuar, ach thuirt Iain gun robh _____ ro bhlàth.

> To Note: it is tempting to put the emphatic pronouns with the word ***fhèin***, which would mirror the way that English puts extra stress on something ("I my*self*" etc.). In practice, most speakers almost never use ***fhèin*** with the emphatic pronouns, and you would be best to avoid it.

Prepositional Pronouns

Over the past few weeks, you have been learning some prepositional pronouns, although you might not have been aware of that. Prepositional pronouns are among the features that identify languages as 'Celtic'. They are also sometimes called 'compound prepositions'. Both names tell you something about what they are: they are compound, or portmanteau words, made out of the merging of prepositions and pronouns. In fact, it may be that thinking of them as 'merging' is inaccurate, as they are an integral feature of very ancient forms of the Celtic languages. In any case, prepositional pronouns are a fundamental feature of Gaelic, and you will have to learn them off by heart as soon as possible.

When ***aig*** is combined with the pronouns, it produces the following forms:

1st person singular	**agam**	at me
2nd person singular	**agad**	at you
3rd person singular (masculine)	**aige**	at him, at it
3rd person singular (feminine)	**aice**	at her, at it
1st person plural	**againn**	at us
2nd person plural	**agaibh**	at you (plural or polite)
3rd person plural	**aca**	at them

A list of the seven forms like this, in this specific order, is known as the **paradigm**. If you learn the **paradigm**, and become completely familiar with what it means, etc., you will find it much easier to learn all of the other prepositional pronouns, as they follow some regular patterns. For instance, the first person plural ('we') ending of every one of the prepositional pronouns is *–inn*, and the second person plural ('you') ending is always *–ibh*. This helps you learn them, as long as you remember the order and understand what it signifies. The **paradigm** of *air* is on the next page:

1st person singular	**orm**	on me
2nd person singular	**ort**	on you
3rd person singular (masculine)	**air**	on him, on it
3rd person singular (feminine)	**oirre**	on her, on it
1st person plural	**oirnn**	on us
2nd person plural	**oirbh**	on you (plural or polite)
3rd person plural	**orra**	on them

You may have noticed that the first person singular form always ends in *–m*. You may also have noticed that the third person singular masculine form often tends to be very similar, or identical, to the preposition itself. The third person singular feminine form is often slender, and the third person plural form is often similar but broad – ***aice/aca***, ***oirre/orra***. Keep these tips in mind when you are memorising the **paradigms** and you will find it an easier task.

Here is the paradigm of ***ann (an)***:

1st person singular	**annam**	in me
2nd person singular	**annad**	in you
3rd person singular (masculine)	**ann**	in him, in it
3rd person singular (feminine)	**innte**	in her, in it
1st person plural	**annainn**	in us
2nd person plural	**annaibh**	in you (plural or polite)
3rd person plural	**annta**	in them

There are **paradigms** of prepositional pronouns for almost all of the simple prepositions. When a preposition is made up of another word and then a preposition (e.g. *faisg air*), you still use these forms:

Faisg orm - near me
Faisg ort - near you
Faisg air - near him, near it
Faisg oirre - near her, near it

Faisg oirnn - near us
Faisg oirbh - near you (pl.)
Faisg orra - near them

Negative Commands

To order somebody not to do something, simply add the word *na* in front of the imperative form:

Na ith sin!
Don't eat that!

Na leugh an leabhar agam!
Don't read my book!

Na bi fadalach!
Don't be late!

Unit 13 Reading Texts:

Bha cù aig Màiri aig an taigh. 'S e Dìleas an t-ainm a bh' air. Bha Dìleas toilichte fad an latha. Bha e toilichte a' falbh a-mach, agus bha e toilichte a' tighinn a-steach. 'S e cù mòr, brèagha a bh' ann. An latha a bha seo, bha Dìleas air bhioran, oir bha Màiri a' tighinn dhachaigh bhon Oilthigh. Ach cha robh Màiri toilichte, oir bha an cnatan oirre. Bha ise ag iarraidh dol don leabaidh le deoch bhlàth. Nuair a bha i a' tighinn a-steach tron doras, chuala i Dìleas a' comhairtich. Choimhead Màiri a-steach anns an taigh, agus chunnaic i Dìleas a' cluich ann. Bha Màiri gu bochd, ach rinn ise gàire nuair a chunnaic i an cù toilichte.

dhachaigh: home
nuair a: when

a' comhairtich: barking

gàire: smile [in Gaelic, you 'do' or 'make' a smile: ***rinn mi gàire***, 'I smiled']

Unit 13 Dialogue:

TIDSEAR: A Chaluim, an do cheannaich thu an leabhar seo?
CALUM: Cha do cheannaich. Cheannaich mi an leabhar sin.
TIDSEAR: Obh obh! Na leugh an leabhar sin. Tha e dona. Leugh an leabhar seo.

Calum stretches across the teacher's desk to look at the book and starts to write down the details

TIDSEAR: Seo. *She hands him the book*
 Tog e.
CALUM: Chan fhaca mi an leabhar seo anns a' bhùth.
TIDSEAR: Coimhead air an ainm. Sgrìobh sin.
CALUM: Rinn mi sin.

He has started to write the ISBN, but his pen stops working

 Obh obh! Chan eil am peann agam ag obair.
TIDSEAR: Tha peann agamsa. Seo. Sgrìobh leis a' pheann seo.
CALUM: Tapadh leibh.

sgrìobh: write

UNIT 14: FUTURE TENSE OF 'TO BE'

Technical Terms Used in this Unit

relative	A part of a sentence that refers to something that has been said already or is about to be said is called **relative** (because it relates to something else).
relative pronoun	A relative pronoun is a 'link word' that joins the sense of two sentences or two bits of sentences together so that they can refer to each other: relative pronouns are words like 'who', 'that', 'which', etc. The relative words are underlined in these examples: 'I spoke to the man who works here'; 'I was very busy yesterday, which explains why I am so tired today'; 'I nearly tripped when I got on the train'. Sometimes relative words (e.g. 'when' in the last example) are no different from conjunctions.
relative form	In the future tense, Gaelic verbs have a special form which appears when they follow a relative pronoun or an interrogative. This is called the relative form.

Faclan an Latha – Your Daily Dose of Vocabulary

Pronouns

a	*which, that, who (relative pronoun)*

Nouns

pàipear-naidheachd (m)	*newspaper*	**am pàipear-naidheachd**	*the newspaper*
pàipearan-naidheachd	*newspapers*	**sa phàipear-naidheachd**	*in the newspaper*
duine (m)	*man, person, anyone*	**an duine**	*the man, the person*
daoine	*men, people*	**aig an duine**	*at the man, at the person*
seachdain (f)	*week*	**an t-seachdain**	*the week*
seachdainean	*weeks*	**san t-seachdain**	*in the week*
		fad na seachdain	*all week*
		deireadh na seachdain	*the weekend*
sgoil (f)	*school*	**an sgoil**	*the school*
sgoiltean	*schools*	**aig an sgoil**	*at school**

Adverbs etc.

a-màireach	*tomorrow*	**Diluain**	*Monday*
		Dimàirt	*Tuesday*

feasgar	*this afternoon, this evening*		
an-ath-seachdain	*next week*	**Diciadain**	*Wednesday*
		Diardaoin	*Thursday*
nuair a	*when* (relative – NOT interrogative)	**Dihaoine**	*Friday*
a-rithist	*again, later*	**Disathairne**	*Saturday*
		Didòmhnaich, Latha na Sàbaid†	*Sunday*

*Note that Gaelic needs the definite article when talking about institutions and institutionalised attendance, where standard English does not (although some dialects, including most Scottish ones, do use the article habitually here).

†Some Gaelic communities are strongly influenced by Christianity, especially Presbyterianism. In some of these areas, the word **Didòmhnaich** is never used, and **Latha na Sàbaid** is favoured instead. In much of Lewis, 'Sunday' is **Latha na Sàbain(d)**.

Future Tense of the Substantive Verb

The future tense of **tha** is **bidh** (with the **–dh** silent in almost all dialects). You use **bidh** in exactly the same ways as **tha** and **bha**:

Bidh mi ag obair a-màireach
I will be working tomorrow

Bidh Seonag aig an taigh feasgar
Joan will be at home this afternoon

Bidh iad toilichte an-ath-sheachdain
They will be happy next week

Eacarsaich 14A. Cuir Gàidhlig air na leanas:

1. Calum will be at school this afternoon.
2. I will be writing a letter to the newspapers.
3. Donald and Joan said that they will be busy working next week.

The negative form of **bidh** is **cha bhi**. You already know that **cha** <u>usually</u> causes lenition if possible, but note that the **–dh** also drops off the end of **bidh** here. This verb has the most eccentric* spelling of any word in the whole Gaelic writing system and so you will simply have to learn how to spell each of the forms as they come up. You use **cha bhi** in exactly the same ways as **chan eil** and **cha robh**.

Bidh mi aig an sgoil a-màireach ach cha bhi duine ann
I'll be at school tomorrow but there won't be anyone there

Cha bhi Sìne sa bhùth idir an-diugh
Jean won't be in the shop at all today

Cha bhi Dàibhidh toilichte nuair a tha fhios aige gu bheil thu an seo
David won't be happy when he knows you are here

Eacarsaich 14B. Cuir Gàidhlig air:

1. I'll be busy all week, but <u>you</u> won't be busy at all.
2. Rory won't be at home tomorrow, and Helen won't be at home on Tuesday.
3. The door won't be open.

The dependent form of **bidh** is **bi**. (Despite the spelling difference, there is really no difference in pronunciation between the two.) The reported/embedded forms are, therefore, **gum bi** and **nach bi**.

Chuala mi gum bi sibh trang aig an sgoil a-màireach
I heard that you'll be busy at school tomorrow

Thuirt Mòrag gum bi i a' leughadh an leabhair sin a-rithist
Morag said that she will be reading that book again

Thuirt Calum nach bi duine ann
Calum said there won't be anyone there

---

*In fact, the spelling of **bi** (etc.) makes perfect sense, but its logic tends to elude very many users of the language. It is, as you know, quite normal for the root (**bi**) of a verb to be shorter than the verbal noun (**bith**). The future tense ending **–dh** is added to the root to form the independent form, **bidh**, and the ending is not added for the dependent form, **bi**. Most people find it easier simply to learn the spellings off by heart, for some reason.

Eacarsaich 14C. Sgrìobh seantansan.

Write two sentences using **gum bi** and two using **nach bi**.

The interrogative form is **am bi**. This works in exactly the same ways as **a bheil** and **an robh**.

> **Other information:**
>
> With most words, the interrogative pre-verb is **an**. However, before a word that begins with **b**, **f**, **m** or **p**, it changes to **am**. This happens because the lips are getting ready to form the verb, and they end up having an influence on the sound of the pre-verb.

Eisimpleirean:

Am bi Tormod sa bhùth feasgar?
Will Norman be in the shop this afternoon?

Am bi sibh ag obair?
Will you be working?

Eacarsaich 14D. Cas mu seach.

Turn the statements in Eacarsaich 14A into questions (e.g. 'Will Calum be at school this afternoon?').

As always, the 'yes' and 'no' answers to direct questions using the interrogative form of the verb are the same as the independent and dependent forms of the verb. So, if the question begins **am bi**, the 'yes' answer will be **bidh** and the 'no' answer will be **cha bhi**. However, some people turn **bidh** into a word with two syllables when they are using it to answer 'yes' (for example when they are giving an emphatic 'yes'). When this happens, the word may be written **bithidh**.

Am bi ... ? - will ... ?
Bidh / bithidh - yes
Cha bhi - no

In the future tense, Gaelic verbs have an extra form, known as the **relative form**. The **relative form** appears when a verb comes after the question words *dè*, *cò*, *ciamar*, *carson*, *cuin*, and also after other words that incorporate **relative pronouns**, such as *ma* (if), and after the **relative pronoun** itself.

The **relative form** of ***bidh*** is ***bhios***.

an duine a bhios
the man who will be

ciamar a bhios ... ?
how will ... be ... ?

cò bhios ... ?
who will be ... ?

dè bhios ... ?
what will be ... ?

ma bhios ...
if ... will be

Notice, though, that the interrogative ***càit(e)*** does not take this form. As with all other verbs and tenses, ***càit(e)*** joins up with the question form of the verb: ***càit am bi thu a' fuireach an-ath-sheachdain?*** = 'where will you be living next week?'

Eacarsaich 14E. Dè a' Bheurla a th' air:

1. Bha mi a' bruidhinn ri duine a bhios aig a' chèilidh a-màireach: bha e air bhioran.
2. Dè bhios tu a' dèanamh aig deireadh na seachdain?
3. Cuin a bhios Màiri a' dol dhachaigh?
4. Cò bhios ag obair sa bhùth?

Here is the paradigm of *do*:

1st person singular	**dhomh**	to me
2nd person singular	**dhut**	to you
3rd person singular (masculine)	**dha**	to him, to it
3rd person singular (feminine)	**dhi**	to her, to it
1st person plural	**dhuinn**	to us
2nd person plural	**dhuibh**	to you (plural or polite)
3rd person plural	**dhaibh**	to them

More Notes on the Dative Case

It is only relatively recently that the indefinite dative has gone out of use, and some writers still use it in very high-register language. The indefinite dative meant nothing for masculine nouns, as they would not change:

balach : aig balach

However, feminine nouns were slenderised where possible:

caileag : aig caileig

You can practise using these old forms in Exercise 7 in the workbook, but no one will expect you to use them outside of the Gaelic class nowadays.

When the preposition **ann (an)** joins up with an article, it becomes **anns an**, **anns a'** or **anns an t-**, as you already know. However, in speech and in informal writing, these are reduced to:

anns an : san
anns a' : sa
anns an t- : san t-

In fact, these forms are also widespread in more formal writing, too, now.

Unit 14 Reading Texts:

Is toil le Calum pàipearan-naidheachd. Tha e trang an-diugh, a-màireach agus Dihaoine, ach bidh e a' leughadh pàipear-naidheachd anns a' mhadainn Disathairne. Bidh e a' leughadh pàipear-naidheachd eile feasgar Disathairne. Bidh e a' leughadh pàipear-naidheachd a-rithist madainn Didòmhnaich, agus bidh e a' leughadh pàipear-naidheachd eile feasgar Didòmhnaich. Is toil le Calum deireadh na seachdain!

eile: another, other

Unit 14 Dialogue:

MÀIRI:	Tha mi sgìth an-diugh.
SORCHA:	Tha mise sgìth cuideachd. Rinn mi cus obair an t-seachdain seo!
MÀIRI:	An toil leat an leabhar seo?
SORCHA:	Cha do leugh mi e.

Màiri hands it to her

MÀIRI:	Seo dhut.
SORCHA:	Tapadh leat.

Sorcha has a look

SORCHA:	Chan fhaca mise an leabhar seo. Tha e a' coimhead glè mhath.
MÀIRI:	Tha e math. Sgrìobh ise leabhar eile cuideachd. Bidh mise a' ceannach an leabhar eile aice a-màireach aig a' bhùth.
SORCHA:	O, am bi? Am bi thu a' dol don bhùth a-màireach?
MÀIRI:	Bithidh. Nach robh fhios agad? Bidh sinn a' ceannach leabhraichean agus ag ithe biadh. Bidh e math.
SORCHA:	Na ceannaich cus! Bidh tu ag iarraidh airgead an-ath-sheachdain cuideachd, nuair a bhios an còmhlan a' cluich ann an Obar Dheathain.
MÀIRI:	Tha sin ceart – bithidh! Am bi thu fhèin a' tighinn ann?
SORCHA:	Bithidh. Is toil leam iad. Cò bhios a' dol don bhùth còmhla riut?
MÀIRI:	Bidh Mairead ann. Cha bhi na balaich a' tighinn còmhla rinn. Cha toil leotha na bùthan. Bidh iadsan san taigh-seinnse.
SORCHA:	Mar as àbhaist!

cuideachd: as well, also
cus: too much, too many
seo dhut: here you are [said when passing something to someone]
còmhlan: band
còmhla ri: with ['with' a person; 'le' tends to be 'with' a thing etc.]
mar as àbhaist: as usual

UNIT 15: NEGATIVE QUESTIONS

Technical Terms Used in this Unit
There are no new technical terms in this unit.

Faclan an Latha – Your Daily Dose of Vocabulary

Prepositions

a [& lenition]	*to*	**dhan** [& dat.]	*to the*

Nouns

dath (m)	*colour*	**an dath**	*the colour*
dathan	*colours*	**leis an dath**	*with the colour*

Adjectives etc.

ùr	*new*		
dearg	*red*	**geal**	*white*
uaine	*green*	**purpaidh**	*purple*
dubh	*black*	**donn**	*brown*
gorm	*blue*	**glas**	*grey*
buidhe	*yellow*	**ruadh**	*red, brown, orange*
liath	*grey, lilac, blue*	**orains**	*orange*
soilleir	*light, bright*	**dorcha**	*dark, dull*

Other information:

The colours in Gaelic do not correspond directly to the colours in English. Although the translations given here will serve you well enough in most contexts, you should be aware that there is a certain amount of overlap in the perception of colours, and that hue and shade are also perceived differently in Gaelic. For instance, ***gorm*** is the everyday word for 'blue', but it is also used for 'green': we would never describe lush grass as ***uaine*** – it would always be ***gorm***. Similarly, although ***dearg*** means 'red', you cannot use it to describe 'red hair': red hair is always ***ruadh***. And, although ***glas*** is the everyday word for 'grey', it never describes hair, which is always ***liath*** when grey. Colours are not really 'adjectives', as such, but they do usually perform the function of adjectives, and they behave like adjectives in Gaelic (e.g. for lenition and slenderising etc.).

So far, you have only been asking positive questions (e.g. 'where <u>do</u> you live?' '<u>did</u> he buy it?' etc.). To ask a negative question in Gaelic, you use the pre-verb **nach**, which you already know as the pre-verb which introduces negative reported speech or embedded clauses. In negative questions, **nach** takes the place of the usual question word (normally, **an** or **am**) or the relative pronoun.

Eisimpleirean:

Nach eil thu sgìth?
Aren't you tired?

Nach e càr ùr a th' ann?
Isn't it a new car?

Nach do sgrìobh i litir?
Didn't she write a letter?

What are the equivalent positive questions to these three examples above?

Barrachd Eisimpleirean:

Carson a dh'òl thu an t-uisge-beatha?
Why did you drink the whisky?

Carson nach do dh'òl thu an t-uisge-beatha?
Why didn't you drink the whisky?

Cuin a bhios tu trang a-màireach?
When will you be busy tomorrow?

Cuin nach bi thu trang a-màireach?
When won't you be busy tomorrow?

Cò tha sgìth?
Who is tired?

Cò nach eil sgìth?

Who isn't tired?

Eacarsaich 15A. Sgrìobh agus cuir ceistean.

1. Write five negative questions using **nach**.
2. Ask your partner your questions.
3. Your partner must make up appropriate answers.

Eacarsaich 15B. Eadar-theangaich na leanas:
SORCHA: Iain, nach do chuir thu an sgudal a-mach fhathast?
IAIN: Cha do chuir: bha mi ro thrang. Nach eil thu fhèin deiseil?
SORCHA: Chan eil: tha mise fhathast ag obair.
IAIN: Nach eil Donnchadh aig an taigh?
SORCHA: Tha, ach tha e sgìth.

sgudal: rubbish, trash

Many prepositions in Gaelic cause lenition on contact with an indefinite noun. This is nothing to do with the dative case, although it can look a bit like the dative case. The preposition *a* ('to') can cause confusion because it is so similar to *à* ('from', 'out of'). However, if you remember that *a* causes lenition and *à* never does, that should help you. Also remember that *a* is usually unstressed and so it is usually pronounced as a central vowel, whereas *à* tends to be stressed and is therefore pronounced as an open vowel.

Eisimpleirean:

Tha mi a' dol a Ghlaschu air a' bhus
I'm going to Glasgow on the bus

Tha mi à Glaschu
I'm from Glasgow

Tha Iain a' dol a Dhùn Èideann
Iain is going to Edinburgh

Here is the paradigm of **bho**:

1st person singular	**bhuam**	from me
2nd person singular	**bhuat**	from you
3rd person singular (masculine)	**bhuaithe**	from him, from it
3rd person singular (feminine)	**bhuaipe**	from her, from it
1st person plural	**bhuainn**	from us
2nd person plural	**bhuaibh**	from you (plural or polite)
3rd person plural	**bhuapa**	from them

Unit 15 Reading Texts:

Tha Màiri agus Sorcha a' dol dhan bhùth an-diugh. Tha Màiri a' dol a cheannach leabhar ùr aig an ùghdar a sgrìobh an leabhar a leugh i an t-seachdain seo. Bidh iad a' falbh aig deich, oir bidh an t-acras air Sorcha anns a' mhadainn, agus bidh i slaodach nuair a bhios i a' dèanamh deiseil. Tha Màiri a' leughadh pàipear-naidheachd an toiseach, oir tha fhios aice gum bi Sorcha slaodach. Tha Sorcha ag ràdh, "Gabh aran ma tha an t-acras ort." Tha Màiri ag ràdh, "Chan eil mi ag iarraidh càil, tapadh leat." Tha Sorcha a' smaoineachadh gu bheil seo ceàrr: "Nach eil an t-acras ort idir?" Tha Màiri a' dèanamh gàire: "Chan eil!"

ùghdar: author
an toiseach: first
ma: if

Unit 15 Dialogue:

Màiri and Sorcha are on the bus, going to the shops. Màiri wants to buy the second book by the author she likes, and Sorcha is hoping to find some other interesting things in the shops.

MÀIRI:	An do dh'ith thu an t-aran air fad, mathà?
SORCHA:	Cha do dh'ith! Na bi mì-mhodhail!

Màiri laughs and looks out the window

MÀIRI:	Tha mi a' smaoineachadh gum bi latha brèagha ann an-diugh.
SORCHA:	Seadh, tha mise a' smaoineachadh gum bi cuideachd.
MÀIRI:	Am faca tu BBC Alba a-raoir?
SORCHA:	Chan fhaca.
MÀIRI:	Nach fhaca? Obh obh! Bha e glè mhath. Bha am balach ud, Iain MacAonghais air. Is toil leam esan.
SORCHA:	An e sin am fear le falt ruadh?
MÀIRI:	Chan e. 'S e sin Dòmhnall Ruadh. Tha falt dorcha donn air Iain.
SORCHA:	O, ceart. Nach eil e à Leòdhas?
MÀIRI:	Tha. Tha mi a' smaoineachadh gu bheil.

An old friend of Sorcha's gets on the bus

CEIT:	Halò, a Shorcha! Is fhada bho nach fhaca mi thu!
SORCHA:	Hai, a Cheit. Ciamar a tha thu?
CEIT:	Tha mi gu dòigheil, tapadh leat. Thu fhèin?
SORCHA:	O, tha mise gu math cuideachd. A Cheit, seo caraid agam, Màiri.
CEIT:	Halò. Ciamar a tha thu?
MÀIRI:	Tha gu math. Cò às a tha thu?
CEIT:	Tha mise às Uibhist, ach tha mi a' fuireach ann an Obar Dheathain fad trì bliadhnaichean a-nis.
SORCHA:	Bha mi fhèin agus Ceit san sgoil còmhla. 'S e nurs a th' innte a-nis.
MÀIRI:	O, glè mhath. Càit a bheil thu ag obair?
CEIT:	Ann an sgoil faisg air seo.
MÀIRI:	O, seadh! Nach eil thu ag obair ann an ospadal?
CEIT:	Chan eil. 'S e nurs sgoile a th' annam. Dè an obair a th' agad fhèin?
MÀIRI:	Tha mi nam oileanach san Oilthigh, còmhla ri Sorcha.

mì-mhodhail: cheeky, rude
falt: hair
còmhla: together

UNIT 16: MORE NOTES ON VERBS

Technical Terms Used in this Unit
There are no new technical terms in this unit.

Faclan an Latha – Your Daily Dose of Vocabulary

Nouns

boireannach (m)	*woman*	**am boireannach**	*the woman*
boireannaich	*women*	**aig a' bhoireannach**	*at the woman*
clann (f) [collective noun]	*children*	**a' chlann**	*the children*
		ris a' chloinn	*to the children*
teaghlach (m)	*family*	**an teaghlach**	*the family*
teaghlaichean	*families*	**aig an teaghlach**	*at the family*
oilthigh (m)	*university*	**an t-oilthigh**	*the university*
oilthighean	*universities*	**san oilthigh**	*in the university*
colaiste (f)	*college*	**a' cholaiste**	*the college*
colaistean	*colleges*	**aig a' cholaiste**	*at the college*
sgoil (f)	*school*	**an sgoil**	*the school*
sgoiltean	*schools*	**san sgoil**	*in the school*
taigh-bìdh (m)	*restaurant*	**an taigh-bìdh**	*the restaurant*
taighean-bìdh	*restaurants*	**aig an taigh-bìdh**	*at the restaurant*

Numbers

dà cheud	*two hundred*
dà cheud gu leth	*two hundred and fifty*
dà cheud, trì fichead 's a deich	*two hundred and seventy*

trì c(h)eud	three hundred
trì c(h)eud 's a h-aon	three hundred and one
seachd ceud, ceithir fichead 's a naoi-deug	seven hundred and ninety-nine
ochd ceud ach aon	seven hundred and ninety-nine
sia fichead	one hundred and twenty
mìle	one thousand

In Unit 12, you encountered the idea that Gaelic verbs have independent and dependent forms. In Unit 14, you learned that the future tense has a third form, the relative form. As you have also seen, the independent, dependent and relative forms are very similar to one another: they are only significantly different in the case of some of the irregular verbs. Here is a reminder of the independent and dependent forms of verbs you know already. The first few are irregular verbs that you have been learning (marked *).

Dependent form:	Independent form:
*A bh<u>eil</u> ... ? Chan <u>eil</u> Gu bh<u>eil</u> Nach <u>eil</u>	Tha
*An e ... ? Chan e Gur e Nach e	'S e
*An <u>tuirt</u> ... ? Cha <u>tuirt</u> Gun <u>tuirt</u> Nach <u>tuirt</u>	Thuirt / thubhairt
*An <u>robh</u> ... ? Cha <u>robh</u> Gun <u>robh</u> Nach <u>robh</u>	Bha
*Am <u>faca</u>...? Chan <u>fhaca</u> Gum <u>faca</u> Nach <u>fhaca</u>	Chunnaic
*An <u>cuala</u>...? Cha <u>chuala</u> Gun <u>cuala</u> Nach <u>cuala</u>	Chuala
*An d' <u>rinn</u>...? Cha d' <u>rinn</u> Gun d' <u>rinn</u>	Rinn

Nach d' rinn	
An do sgrìobh...? Cha do sgrìobh Gun do sgrìobh Nach do sgrìobh	Sgrìobh
An do thog...? Cha do thog Gun do thog Nach do thog	Thog
An do fhreagair...? Cha do fhreagair Gun do fhreagair Nach do fhreagair	Fhreagair
An do dh'fhuirich...? Cha do dh'fhuirich Gun do dh'fhuirich Nach do dh'fhuirich	Dh'fhuirich
An do dh'òl...? Cha do dh'òl Gun do dh'òl Nach do dh'òl	Dh'òl

Notice that the only difference between the independent and dependent forms in the past tense of regular verbs is that the dependent form is preceded by ***do***.

The only verb you have seen in the future tense so far is the substantive verb, and you know that, in addition to the independent and dependent forms, it also includes a relative form.

Dependent form	Independent form	Relative form
Am bi...? **Cha bhi** **Gum bi** **Nach bi**	**Bidh / Bithidh**	**Bhios**

With simple questions asked using the interrogative part of the verb (i.e. the **an** or **am** form), the 'yes' answer is always the same as the independent form, and the 'no' answer is always the same as the dependent form (with **cha(n)**).

An do dh'òl thu an t-uisge-beatha air fad?
Did you drink all the whisky?

Dh'òl.
Yes.

A bheil...?
is, am, are?
Tha
yes
Chan eil
no

An robh...?
was, were?
Bha
yes
Cha robh
no

An e...?
is, am, are?
'S e
yes
Chan e
no

Am bi...?
will...be?
Bidh
yes
Cha bhi
no

An do sgrìobh?
did ... write?
Sgrìobh
yes
Cha do sgrìobh
no

An d' rinn?
did ... do?
Rinn
yes
Cha d' rinn
no

An cuala...?
did ... hear?
Chuala
yes
Cha chuala
no

Notice that this rule holds true even with the irregular verbs and the highly irregular auxiliary verbs, the copula and the substantive.

Eacarsaich 16. Consolidation.

Copy the table above, with its two columns (dependent and independent) and fill in all the other verbs you know: e.g.

Dependent	Independent
An do dh'ith ...?	**Dh'ith**
Cha do dh'ith	
Gun do dh'ith	
Nach do dh'ith	

Here is the list again:

bruidhinn	-	bruidhinn
ceannachd	-	ceannaich
cluich	-	cluich
coimhead	-	coimhead
danns	-	danns

dràibheadh	-	dràibh
èisteachd	-	èist
falbh	-	falbh
freagairt	-	freagair
fuireach	-	fuirich
gabhail	-	gabh
ithe	-	ith
leughadh	-	leugh
obair	-	obair
òl	-	òl
peantadh	-	peant
reic	-	reic
seinn	-	seinn
sgioblachadh	-	sgioblaich
sgrìobhadh	-	sgrìobh
siubhal	-	siubhail
smaoineachadh	-	smaoinich
snàmh	-	snàmh
tachairt	-	tachair
togail	-	tog

Here is the paradigm of *le*:

1st person singular	**leam**	with me
2nd person singular	**leat**	with you
3rd person singular (masculine)	**leis**	with him, with it
3rd person singular (feminine)	**leatha**	with her, with it
1st person plural	**leinn**	with us
2nd person plural	**leibh**	with you (plural or polite)
3rd person plural	**leotha**	with them

Unit 16 Reading Texts:

Bhruidhinn mi ri Calum aig a' cholaiste an-dè. Thuirt e gun do sgrìobh e aiste airson Gearmailtis, ach cha robh e toilichte leatha. Bha e a' smaoineachadh gun d' rinn e mearachdan innte. Ach, chuala mi nach do sgrìobh Anna aiste idir: tha sin dona, nach eil! Dh'fhuirich mi aig a' cholaiste airson biadh. Tha taigh-bìdh math ann. Dh'ith mi gu leòr, ach cha do dh'òl mi càil, oir chan eil deochannan math aca, agus cha toil leam uisge. Thog mi na leabhraichean agam, agus dh'fhalbh mi dhan bhùth-leabhraichean san t-Sràid Mhòir. Cheannaich mi faclair ùr, ach cha do cheannaich mi pinn, oir tha gu leòr pinn agam. Leugh mi an leabhar ùr air a' bhus, nuair a bha mi a' tighinn dhachaigh.

aiste: essay
airson: for
mearachd(an): mistake(s)
faclair: dictionary

Unit 16 Dialogue:

The bus stops near the shops. Màiri and Sorcha say goodbye to Ceit

NIGHEANAN: Tioraidh an-dràsta!
CEIT: Tioraidh! Chì mi rithist sibh!

Sorcha looks in the window of the shoe shop

SORCHA: Hei, a Mhàiri! Seall sin! Is toil leam na brògan sin!
MÀIRI: Tha iad brèagha. Ach dà cheud not, a Shorcha!
SORCHA: Tha fhios a'm.... ach seall cho brèagha 's a tha iad...
MÀIRI: A bheil dà cheud not agad idir?
SORCHA: Chan eil an t-airgead sin leam, ach tha e agam aig an taigh.
MÀIRI: Aig an taigh?! Carson nach eil e anns a' bhanca?
SORCHA: Cha toil leam bancaichean.

seall: look
bròg(an): shoe(s)

UNIT 17: THE FUTURE TENSE

Technical Terms Used in this Unit

syncope The loss of an internal syllable. This is usually caused in Gaelic when an ending is added to a word, making it more difficult to pronounce. It happens in the relative form of some verbs in the future tense. You have also seen it happening when some nouns became plural: e.g. *litir* : *litrichean*. Syncope can only happen to an unstressed syllable.

Faclan an Latha – Your Daily Dose of Vocabulary

Verbs

a' cluich	*playing*	**a' cadal**	*sleeping*
cluich!	*play!*	**cadail!**	*sleep!*
ag èisteachd (ri)	*listening (to)*	**a' dùsgadh**	*waking up*
èist!	*listen*	**dùisg!**	*wake up!*
a' sgrìobhadh	*writing*	**a' coimhead (air)**	*looking, watching*
sgrìobh!	*write!*	**coimhead!**	*look!*
a' leughadh	*reading*		
leugh!	*read!*		

Nouns

latha (m)	*day*	**an latha**	*the day*
làithean	*days*	**tron latha**	*through the day*
		fad an latha	*all day*
madainn (f)	*morning*	**a' mhadainn**	*the morning*
maidnean	*mornings*	**sa mhadainn**	*in the morning*
		sa mhadainn an-diugh	*this morning*
		fad na maidne	*all morning*
feasgar (m)	*afternoon, evening*	**am feasgar**	*the afternoon*
feasgaran	*afternoons, evenings*	**san fheasgar**	*in the afternoon*

		feasgar an-dè	*yesterday afternoon*
		fad an fheasgair	*all afternoon*
oidhche (f)	*night*	**an oidhche**	*the night*
oidhcheannan	*nights*	**air an oidhche**	*at night*
		fad na h-oidhche	*all night*

Adjectives

math	*good*
dona	*bad*
fada	*long*
goirid	*short*
brèagha	*pretty*
grànna	*ugly*
trom	*heavy*
aotrom	*light*

The future tense of regular verbs (i.e. almost all verbs in the language) is formed according to a small set of predictable patterns. The only additional complication compared to the past tense is that the future tense includes a relative form. The relative form of regular verbs is similar to the relative form of the substantive verb which you saw in Unit 14.

To make the future tense, you need the root of the verb.

Here are the verbal nouns and roots we used when making the past tense:

bruidhinn	-	bruidhinn
ceannachd	-	ceannaich
cluich	-	cluich
coimhead	-	coimhead
danns	-	danns
dràibheadh	-	dràibh
èisteachd	-	èist
falbh	-	falbh
freagairt	-	freagair
fuireach	-	fuirich
gabhail	-	gabh
ithe	-	ith
leughadh	-	leugh
obair	-	obair
òl	-	òl
peantadh	-	peant

reic	-	reic
seinn	-	seinn
sgioblachadh	-	sgioblaich
sgrìobhadh	-	sgrìobh
siubhal	-	siubhail
smaoineachadh	-	smaoinich
snàmh	-	snàmh
tachairt	-	tachair
togail	-	tog

1. To make the independent form, add the ending *–(a)idh*.

Sgrìobh!
Write!

Sgrìobhaidh
Will write

Sgrìobhaidh mi litir a-màireach
I'll write a letter tomorrow

Tog!
Lift!

Togaidh
Will lift

Togaidh mi an leabhar
I'll lift the book

Adding this ending could cause some words to be rather long or unnecessarily difficult to pronounce. Therefore, Gaelic has developed a process called **syncope**, which allows a middle vowel to be cropped out of the word when an ending is added. This happens with the verb ***bruidhinn***.

Bruidhinn!
Speak!

Bruidhnidh mi
I'll speak

Bruidhnidh mi ri Màiri an-ath-sheachdain
I'll speak to Mary next week

Notice that the future tense ending finishes in **–dh**. When the pronoun ***thu*** follows **–dh-**, it becomes ***tu***.

Leughaidh tu an litir
You'll read the letter

2. To make the dependent form, simply use the root as it is.

Ith!
Eat!

An ith...?
Will ... eat?

An ith thu sin?
Will you eat that?

Cuir!
Put!

An cuir?
Will ... put?

An cuir sinn an càr sa gharaids?

Will we put the car in the garage?

3. To make the relative form, lenite the root if possible (or add **dh'** to vowels) and add the ending *-(e)as*.

Ceannaich!
Buy!

Cheannaichas
[rel.] *will buy*

Cò cheannaicheas peann ùr dhomh?
Who will buy a new pen for me?

Smaoinich!
Think!

Smaoinicheas
[rel.] *will think*

Cuin a smaoinicheas Iain?
When will Iain think?

Freagair!
Answer!

Fhreagras
[rel.] *will answer*

Ciamar a fhreagras tu?
How will you answer?

Did you notice the **syncope** in the last example?

Negative questions always take the dependent form and NOT the relative form. This is because they include the word **nach**, which must take the dependent form.

Carson nach freagair thu?
Why won't you answer?

Cò nach òl uisge-beatha?
Who won't drink whisky?

Dè nach leugh thu?
What won't you read?

Dependent	Independent	Relative
an leugh...? **cha leugh** **gun leugh** **nach leugh**	**leughaidh**	**leughas**
an cuir ... ? **cha chuir** **gun cuir** **nach cuir**	**cuiridh**	**chuireas**
am freagair ...? **cha fhreagair** **gum freagair / gun fhreagair** **nach fhreagair / nach freagair**	**freagraidh**	**fhreagras**

am fuirich ...? chan fhuirich gum fuirich nach fhuirich / nach fuirich	fuirichidh	dh'fhuiricheas
an òl ...? chan òl gun òl nach òl	òlaidh	dh'òlas

Remember that the question words **dè**, **cò**, **cuin**, **ciamar**, and **carson** all take the relative form in the future tense. However, the question word **càit** always takes the question form of a verb:

Eisimpleirean:

Cò dh'òlas an t-uisge-beatha?
Ciamar a dh'òlas tu an t-uisge-beatha?
Cuin a dh'òlas Seonag an t-uisge-beatha?
Dè dh'òlas Iain?
Carson a dh'òlas Màiri an t-uisge-beatha?
Càit an òl mi an t-uisge-beatha?

Eacarsaich 17. Sgrìobhadh.

Write twelve sentences using verbs in the future tense. Make sure some are:

1. positive, (b) negative, (c) verbs that start with a lenitable consonant, (d) verbs that start with a vowel.

Unit 17 Reading Texts:
Bidh Màrtainn glè thoilichte an-ath-sheachdain, nuair a bhios e aig an taigh.

Bruidhnidh e ris an teaghlach aige, cluichidh e an giotàr aige, agus seinnidh e còmhla ris a chàirdean anns a' chòmhlan. An leugh e an leabhar aige airson an Oilthigh? Is dòcha gun leugh, ach is dòcha nach leugh: cò aige tha fios? Ach, tha fios gun ith e mòran, gun òl e mòran, agus gum bi spòrs aige. Bha e a' dol a reic an càr aige, ach cha reic e sin fhathast. Cumaidh e an càr an-dràsta. Thuirt e gun sgrìobh e gu Sìle nuair a bhios e aig an taigh, ach cha sgrìobh: bidh e ro thrang, agus cha bhi cuimhne aige.

is dòcha: maybe [takes the embedded/reported form]
mòran: a lot
spòrs: fun
a' cumail; cùm!: keeping, keep!

Unit 17 Dialogue:
Sorcha and Màiri are still at the shops

SORCHA: Seall am baga sin! An ceannaich mi e?
MÀIRI: A Shorcha! Dè mu dheidhinn na brògan?
SORCHA: Bidh iad brèagha còmhla, nach bi?
MÀIRI: A Shorcha, tha na brògan ud a' cosg dà cheud not. Tha am baga fhèin trì fichead 's a deich. Ma cheannaicheas tu na brògan **agus** am baga, cosgaidh sin dà cheud, trì fichead 's a deich notaichean. Pàighidh sin màl dhut airson trì seachdainean.
SORCHA: Is dòcha gum pàigh, ach cha bhi am baga seo agam. Tha mi ag iarraidh seo.
MÀIRI: Am fuirich thu gus am bi do mhàthair an seo? Ceannaichidh ise am baga dhut.
SORCHA: Chan fhuirich. Reicidh iad na brògan agus am baga, agus cha cheannaich mo mhàthair càil dhomh. Cleachdaidh mi a' chairt-chreideis agam.
MÀIRI: Chan èist thu rium idir, an èist?
SORCHA: **Tha** mi ag èisteachd... ach ceannaichidh mi na brògan 's am baga!

mu dheidhinn: about
a' cosg: costing, spending, wasting
not(aichean): pound(s)
a' pàigheadh: paying
màl: rent
a' cleachdadh: using
cairt-creideis: credit card

UNIT 18: EXPRESSING POSSESSION AND OWNERSHIP

Technical Terms Used in this Unit
There are no new technical terms in this unit.

Faclan an Latha – Your Daily Dose of Vocabulary

Key Words and Expressions

is toil leam...	*I like...*	**is toil le Màiri...**	*Mary likes...*
an toil leat...?	*do you like...?*	**... gur toil le Iain ...**	*... that Iain likes ...*
cha toil leam...	*I don't like...*	**... nach toil le Iain ...**	*... that Iain doesn't like...*

Verbs

a' smèideadh (ri)	*waving (to)*	**a' ceannach(d)**	*buying*
smèid!	*wave!*	**ceannaich!**	*buy!*
a' gabhail ri	*accepting*	**a' freagairt**	*answering*
gabh ri...!	*accept!*	**freagair!**	*answer!*
a' bruidhinn (ri)	*speaking (to)*	**a' seinn**	*singing*
bruidhinn!	*speak!*	**seinn!***	*sing!*

Prepositions

còmhla ri	*(along) with*

* The idiomatic way to tell somebody to sing a song, though, is **gabh òran** [lit. 'take a song'].

You already know that there is no verb 'to have' in Gaelic, and that the normal way to express possession is to use the preposition *aig*, 'at': **tha taigh ùr aig Iain** - 'Iain has a new house'. When it is necessary to emphasise that possession is more permanent – e.g. when ownership must be established – the preposition used is *le*, 'with'. Most commonly, this preposition is used with the copula. As you know, the copula is used for defining and identifying, and it is also used for being emphatic. For joining *le* to the copula, a special construction is needed (***'s ann le***). This construction is explored further in the next unit, so just learn it as vocabulary for the moment.

'S ann le Marsaili a tha an leabhar sin
That book is Marsaili's / That book belongs to Marsaili

'S ann le Seònaid a tha an taigh a tha faisg air a' bhùth
Janet owns the house which is near the shop

'S ann le Teàrlach a tha am peann mòr gorm sin
That big blue pen belongs to Charles

If the thing in question belongs to someone who is not named (e.g. 'a boy', 'the girl' etc.), then the usual dative case rules come into play. If the noun is indefinite, then the preposition remains *le*:

'S ann le balach beag a tha an càr
The car belongs to a little boy

If the noun is definite (singular), *le* becomes *leis* as usual:

'S ann leis a' bhalach bheag sin a tha an dèideag
The toy belongs to that little boy

Of course, with definite plural nouns, *le* does not need to change:

'S ann le na daoine cudromach a tha sin
That belongs to the important people

Other information:

The matter of **le** changing to **leis** when it is followed by **na** is a controversial one among speakers. Some speakers would say and write **leis na**. This is just as acceptable as **le na**.

The negative version of this expression is **chan ann le**:

Chan ann le Mairead a tha am peann sin
That isn't Margaret's pen

Chan ann leis an duine mhòr a tha e
It doesn't belong to the big man

The question form is **an ann le**:

An ann le Dùghall a tha an leabhar dearg?
Is the red book Doug's?

An ann le caileag a tha am bàta?
Does the boat belong to a girl?

To answer the **an ann le** question, simply use the positive or negative forms as usual:

An ann le ... a tha ... ?

'S ann
yes

Chan ann
no

The indirect speech forms are based on the copula, too: **gur ann** and **nach ann**. So, for instance:

Tha mi a' smaoineachadh gur ann le Ealasaid a tha an t-uisge-beatha
I think the whisky belongs to Elizabeth

Chuala mi nach ann le Seonag a tha an càr gorm
I heard that the blue car is not Joan's

Eacarsaich 18A. Cuir Gàidhlig air:

1. Is it Norman's big pen?
2. No, it's Calum's; Norman has a little pen.
3. The boat belongs to Jean.
4. The book doesn't belong to Marsaili; it belongs to Donald.

Here is the paradigm of *ri*:

1st person singular	**rium**	to me
2nd person singular	**riut**	to you
3rd person singular (masculine)	**ris**	to him, to it
3rd person singular (feminine)	**rithe**	to her, to it
1st person plural	**rinn**	to us
2nd person plural	**ribh**	to you (plural or polite)
3rd person plural	**riutha**	to them

Eacarsaich 18B. Cuir Gàidhlig air:

1. saying to me
2. talking to her
3. along with us
4. listening to him
5. wait for me
6. waving to you (pl.)
7. accepting it
8. talking to them
9. along with her
10. waiting for you

Unit 18 Reading Texts:

Tha càr mòr ùr air an t-sràid againn. 'S ann le Dùghlas a tha e. Smaoinich mi gur ann le Mìchel a bha e, ach bha mise ceàrr: chan ann leis-san a tha e idir. Is toil leam gu mòr an càr ùr aig Dùghlas. Thuirt Ciorstaidh nach toil leatha e, ach tha mise a' smaoineachadh nach eil sin fìor: tha mise a' smaoineachadh gur toil leatha e, ach gu bheil i beagan farmadach. Bruidhinn mi ri Dùghlas mun chàr ùr aige. Bha e toilichte gur toil leam an càr. Thuirt e gun tog e mi a-màireach anns a' chàr.

fìor: true
farmadach: jealous

Unit 18 Dialogue:

Gòrdan, Niall and Calum have had a late night in the pub. They are tired and hungry

GÒRDAN: Tha ceann goirt orm.
NIALL: Dh'òl thu cus a-raoir.
GÒRDAN: Dh'òl agus thusa.
NIALL: Tha sin fìor. Càit a bheil Calum?
GÒRDAN: Chan eil fhios a'm. Cha do dhùisg mi ach an-dràsta.

They find Calum sleeping on the floor in the kitchen

CALUM: Obh obh! Mo cheann! Càit a bheil mi?
GÒRDAN: Tha thu sa chidsin, a bhalaich.
CALUM: Seadh, agus cò thusa?
GÒRDAN: Is mise Gòrdan. Tha mi anns a' chlas Ghàidhlig agad. Nach eil cuimhne agad?
CALUM: A bheil mise a' dèanamh clas Gàidhlig?
GÒRDAN: Tha. San Oilthigh.
CALUM: Oilthigh? Obh obh!

Niall opens the fridge door and pulls out a milk carton

NIALL: Cò leis a tha seo?
CALUM: Cò aige tha fios?
GÒRDAN: Uill, chan ann leamsa a tha e: chan eil mise a' fuireach an seo.
NIALL: An ann leatsa a tha e, a Chaluim?
CALUM: Chan ann. Tha mi a' smaoineachadh gur ann leatsa a tha e. Dèan cofaidh

	co-dhiù!
NIALL:	O. Cò leis a tha an cofaidh?
CALUM:	'S ann leamsa a tha e, ach dèan cofaidh dhuinn uile. Tha mise a' fuireach an seo air an làr airson greis, ma tha sin ceart gu leòr.

ceann: head
goirt: sore
cò leis: whose
co-dhiù: anyway
làr: floor
airson greis: for a while
ceart gu leòr: ok

UNIT 19: THE COPULA FOR EMPHASIS

Technical Terms Used in this Unit

fronting	moving an element leftwards in the sentence in order to emphasise it
clefting / cleft structure	emphasising an element in a sentence by means of fronting

Faclan an Latha – Your Daily Dose of Vocabulary

Verbs

a' coiseachd	*walking*	**ag èirigh**	*getting up*
coisich!	*walk!*	**èirich!**	*get up!*
a' ruith	*running*	**a' cur**	*putting, planting, sending*
ruith!	*run!*		
		cuir!	*put! plant! send!*

Adjectives etc.

blàth	*warm*	**air** [possessive pronoun] **s(h)ocair**	*at ease*
		air mo shocair	*at my ease, at my leisure*
àrd	*high, tall*	**gabh air do shocair!**	*take it easy!*
socair	*quiet, peaceful*		
luath	*fast*		
slaodach	*slow*		
snog	*nice*		
ìseal	*low*		

Nouns

saoghal (m)	*world*	**an saoghal**	*the world*
saoghail	*worlds*	**san t-saoghal**	*in the world*

teine (m)	*fire*	**an teine**	*the fire*
teintean	*fires*	**san teine***	*in the fire*

* Until relatively recently, ***teine*** had an irregular dative form, and you may still come across it: ***teinidh***.

In the previous unit, you learned how to express long-term possession or ownership using the idiom **'s ann le**. This consists of the copula **is** (in its common, abbreviated form), the preposition **ann** (which we often see as **ann an**) and the preposition **le**.

> Note that some of the English translations in this unit are very questionable English, but they are designed to give fairly literal versions of the Gaelic sentences so that you can see how the emphasising works.

As you know, the copula is used for identifying things ('it is a ...'; 'he is James'), for defining ('he is a lorry driver'; 'it is a green one') and also for emphasising things. When you are emphasising a noun or pronoun, you normally use one of the structures we have already been using:

'S e ...
'S e ... a th' ann
'S esan ...

There will be more information on this in later units.

Emphasising something other than a noun or pronoun requires a special construction: **'s ann ... (a tha ...)**. This construction is used for emphasising verbs, adverbs, adjectives, prepositional structures etc.

'S ann a-màireach a bhios e a' tighinn
It's <u>tomorrow</u> that he'll be coming

'S ann a' dannsa a bha i
It's <u>dancing</u> that she was / she was <u>dancing</u>

'S ann air a' bhus a chunnaic mi e
It's <u>on the bus</u> that I saw him

'S ann an-diugh a tha mi gu h-àraidh trang
It's <u>today</u> that I'm especially busy

'S ann trang a tha mi an-diugh
It's <u>busy</u> that I am today

As you will have noticed in the last two examples, it is possible to change the element in the sentence that is being emphasised, just by moving it closer to the **'s ann** part. We call this **fronting** or **clefting**. It is exactly the same as emphasising a noun by bringing it leftwards beside **'s e**.

As you would expect, the negative version is **chan ann**, and the question form is **an ann?** The indirect forms are **gur ann** and **nach ann**. In other words, this is exactly the same construction that we used with **le** in the previous unit.

Remember that, when you ask a question that begins **an ann ...** the 'yes' answer is **'s ann** and the 'no' answer is **chan ann**.

An ann sa bhùth a tha thu?
Chan ann; 's ann aig an taigh a tha mi an-dràsta.

Is it <u>at the shop</u> that you are?
No; I'm <u>at home</u> just now.

An ann ag obair a tha Sìne?
'S ann: tha i glè thrang.

Is it <u>working</u> that Jean is?
Yes: she's very busy.

Here are examples of the indirect or embedded forms working:

Chuala mi gur ann an-dè a sgrìobh Anndra an litir.
I heard that it was <u>yesterday</u> that Andrew wrote the letter.

Thuirt Iain nach ann aig a' chèilidh a bha e.
Iain said that it was not <u>at the ceilidh</u> that he was.

This construction is for emphasising things. You may be able to give the same <u>information</u> in a different way. Consider:

A bheil thu à Fionnlainn?
Are you from Finland?

An ann à Fionnlainn a tha thu?
Is it from <u>Finland</u> that you are?

In the first example, the speaker is just looking for information. In the second, he/she is confirming something that may be in some doubt.

Eacarsaich 19. A' cur cuideam air.

Write short sentences, emphasising the following:

1. ag obair
2. an-diugh
3. an-dè
4. aig an taigh
5. san sgoil
6. a' sgrìobhadh litir
7. à Canada
8. le Mòrag

Here is the paradigm of *de*:

1st person singular	**dhìom**	off/from me
2nd person singular	**dhìot**	off/from you
3rd person singular (masculine)	**dheth**	off/from him, off/from it
3rd person singular (feminine)	**dhith**	off/from her, off/from it
1st person plural	**dhinn**	off/from us
2nd person plural	**dhibh**	off/from you (plural or polite)
3rd person plural	**dhiubh**	off/from them

Unit 19 Reading Texts:

Tha Eòghann à Glaschu, ach chan ann ann an sin a tha e a' fuireach an-dràsta: 's ann ann an Dùn Èideann a tha e a' fuireach. 'S e oileanach a th' ann. Chan ann aig an Oilthigh fhèin a tha e a' fuireach: 's ann faisg air Sràid a' Phrionnsa a tha e a' fuireach. Chan ann leis fhèin a tha an taigh anns a bheil e a' fuireach: 's ann le uncail a tha an taigh, agus mar sin chan eil Eòghann a' pàigheadh mòran màl. Cha robh e a' dèanamh mòran obair nuair a bha e san sgoil, ach 's ann a tha e ag obair gu cruaidh a-nis!

uncail: uncle
mar sin: therefore
cruaidh: hard

Unit 19 Dialogue:

Gòrdan, Calum and Niall are late for their class

NIALL: Dè an uair a tha e?
GÒRDAN: Chan eil fhios a'm: faisg air deich, is dòcha.

Calum picks up his phone and checks the time

CALUM: Chan eil! 'S ann a tha e faisg air aon uair deug! Tha sinn gu bhith fadalach!
NIALL: Obh obh! Cha choisich sinn dhan Oilthigh ro aon uair deug: 's ann ro fhada a tha e.
GÒRDAN: Cleachdaidh sinn am bus. Tha am bus a' ruith dhan Oilthigh bhon a seo.
CALUM: Tha, ach chan e am bus ceart a bhios ann an-dràsta. 'S e am bus aig meadhan-latha a bhios a' dol dhan Oilthigh. Chan ann dhan Oilthigh a tha am bus sin a' dol idir.
GÒRDAN: Is dòcha nach ann, ach nach eil e a' dol suas Sràid an Rìgh?
NIALL: Tha. Ma ruitheas sinn bho Shràid an Rìgh, bidh sinn ceart gu leòr! Sin thu fhèin, a Ghòrdain!

gu bhith: almost, about to be
meadhan-latha: midday
sin thu fhèin!: well done!

UNIT 20: THE INFINITIVE

Technical Terms Used in this Unit
There are no new technical terms in this unit.

Faclan an Latha – Your Daily Dose of Vocabulary

Nouns

bus (m)	bus	**am bus**	the bus
busaichean	buses	**air a' bhus**	on the bus
plèan (m)	plane	**am plèan**	the plane
plèanaichean	planes	**air a' phlèan**	on the plane
bàta (m)	boat	**am bàta**	the boat
bàtaichean	boats	**air a' bhàta**	on the boat
trèan (f)	train	**an trèan**	the train
trèanaichean	trains	**air an trèan**	on the train

Verbs

a' seòladh	sailing	**a' fosgladh**	opening
seòl!	sail!	**fosgail!**	open!
a' suidhe	sitting	**a' dùnadh**	closing
suidh!	sit!	**dùin!**	close!
ag innse	telling	**a' cumail**	keeping
innis!	tell!	**cùm!**	keep!
a' cleachdadh	using	**a' briseadh**	breaking
cleachd!	use!	**bris!**	break!
a' glanadh	cleaning	**ag ionnsachadh**	learning
glan!	clean!	**ionnsaich!**	learn!

More Nouns

corp (m)	*body*	**an corp**	*the body*
cuirp	*bodies*	**sa chorp**	*in the body*
aodann (m)	*face*	**an t-aodann**	*the face*
aodainn	*faces*	**air an aodann**	*on the face*
ceann (m)	*head*	**an ceann**	*the head*
cinn	*heads*	**air a' cheann**	*on the head*
sùil (f)	*eye*	**an t-sùil**	*the eye*
sùilean	*eyes*	**san t-sùil**	*in the eye*
sròn (f)	*nose*	**an t-sròn**	*the nose*
sròintean	*noses*	**san t-sròin**	*in the nose*
cluas (f)	*ear*	**a' chluas**	*the ear*
cluasan	*ears*	**sa chluais**	*in the ear*

There is no proper infinitive form in Gaelic, but a version of the verbal noun is used to perform some of the function of an infinitive, and many Gaelic teachers simply call this the infinitive for the sake of convenience. So far, when you have been using the verbal noun, it has been preceded by the preposition **ag** (or **a'** before a consonant). This is a shortened form of **aig** ('at'), and it conveys the sense that the verb is in progress. When the preposition **a** ('to') is added to the verbal noun instead, it gives us the sense of 'to' do something:

a' sgrìobhadh
writing [ongoing, continuing]

a sgrìobhadh
to write

ag ràdh
saying

a ràdh
to say

Remember that **a** causes lenition:

a' ceannachd
buying

a cheannachd
to buy

a' dol
going

a dhol
to go

Remember that, although vowels do not lenite, they sometimes acquire **dh'** in situations where consonants would lenite:

ag ithe
eating

a dh'ithe
to eat

ag obair
working

a dh'obair
to work

> **Other information:**
>
> The preposition **a** is actually a version of **do**, which has been de-emphasised over the centuries. This is why it causes lenition (because **do** always causes lenition). The **dh'** which is added to words that start with vowels is also a manifestation of **do**. So, when we write **do dh'Ìle** or **a dh'Ìle**, we are actually doubling up the preposition. The same kind of thing happened to **an** and turned it into **ann an**.

Eacarsaich 20A. Cuir Gàidhlig air:

1. I'm going to eat porridge every day.
2. Janet is going to write a letter.
3. Are they going to work all day?
4. Norman isn't going to buy anything tomorrow.

Did you notice that 'going to' with a verbal noun is very similar to 'going to' with a noun?

Tha mi a' dol a Ghlaschu
I'm going to Glasgow

Tha mi a' dol a ghabhail...
I'm going to take...

Tha mi a' dol a dh'Ìle
I'm going to Islay

Tha mi a' dol a dh'ithe
I'm going to eat

The verbs ***tighinn*** and ***sgur*** also take this construction:

Tha Màiri a' tighinn a dh'obair feasgar
Mary is coming to work this afternoon

A bheil Iain a' tighinn a dh'fhosgladh an dorais?
Is Iain coming to open the door?

Chan eil a' chlann a' sgur a bhruidhinn
The children aren't stopping speaking

Thuirt Calum gu bheil e a' sgur a sgrìobhadh leabhraichean
Calum said that he is stopping writing books

Notice that when ***sgur*** takes this construction the normal English translation is not 'stopping to', but just 'stopping'.

Here is the paradigm of ***ro***:

1st person singular	**romham**	before me
2nd person singular	**romhad**	before you
3rd person singular (masculine)	**roimhe**	before him, before it
3rd person singular (feminine)	**roimhpe**	before her, before it
1st person plural	**romhainn**	before us
2nd person plural	**romhaibh**	before you (plural or polite)
3rd person plural	**romhpa**	before them

Unit 20 Reading Texts:

'S e am bàta *Eileanan Innse Gall* a bhios a' seòladh a dh'Ìle. 'S e seann bhàta mòr a th' anns na h-*Eileanan Innse Gall*. Thog Cochrane Shipbuilders am bàta ann an 1985, ach tha e fhathast math. Tha na h-*Eileanan Innse Gall* a' dol a sheòladh a dh'Ìle a-màireach aig seachd sa mhadainn. Ma tha thu ag iarraidh a dhol ann, ceannaich ticead bho Chalmac. Nuair a sguireas na h-*Eileanan Innse Gall* a sheòladh, bidh mòran dhaoine glè bhrònach. Tha e furasta a dhol a dh'Ìle ann am plèan cuideachd, ach cha toil leis a h-uile duine plèanaichean.

seann: old
ticead: ticket
Calmac: Caledonian MacBrayne, the ferry operator
brònach: sad
furasta: easy

Unit 20 Dialogue:

Sorcha and Màiri have spent a lot of money at the shops and they are both feeling a bit nervous about it

SORCHA: A bheil sinn a' dol a dh'ithe a-nis?
MÀIRI: A bheil airgead againn fhathast?
SORCHA: Chan eil mi cinnteach. Chan eil mi ag iarraidh a choimhead air inneal a' bhanca.
MÀIRI: A bheil thu a' dol a chumail na brògan agus am baga?
SORCHA: 'S ann leamsa a tha iad a-nis. Tha mi a' dol a dh'obair san taigh-seinnse gach deireadh na seachdain. Bidh mi ceart gu leòr.
MÀIRI: Uill, tha an t-acras orm an-dràsta. Càit a bheil sinn a' dol?
SORCHA: Tha an taigh-bìdh seo math.

As they approach the restaurant, a young man hurries to open the door for them from inside

SORCHA: Seall am balach ud! Nach e a tha eireachdail!
MÀIRI: 'S e gu dearbh! 'S ann brèagha a tha na sùilean aige.
SORCHA: Chan ann air na sùilean a bha mise a' coimhead!

BALACH: Feasgar math, a nigheanan. O mo chreach! Abair bròganagus baga brèagha! Càit an do cheannaich thu iad?
SORCHA: Obh obh!

cinnteach: sure
inneal a' bhanca: the bank machine (ATM)
gu dearbh: indeed, certainly
mo chreach!: oh goodness!
abair: say [used to exclaim whatever follows – e.g. 'abair gu bheil mi sgìth!']

UNIT 21: IRREGULAR VERBS AND POSSESSIVE PRONOUNS

Technical Terms Used in this Unit

auxiliary verb
An auxiliary verb is one that is used to provide structure to a sentence, without really meaning much in its own right. In English, the auxiliary verb 'do' stands in for a present tense: 'Do you eat fish and chips?' 'Yes, I do'.

eclipsis
A sound change that involves the beginning of a word being dropped or modified because of the word that comes before it. When the *s* at the beginning of a noun is preceded by *t-*, the /s/ sound disappears in favour of the /t/, and we call this eclipsis.

Faclan an Latha ... Your Daily Dose of Vocabulary

Key Words and Phrases

tha an t-acras orm	*I'm hungry*
tha am pathadh orm	*I'm thirsty*

Adjectives, Adverbials, Intensifiers, Modifiers

tràth	*early*	**cho**	*so, as*
fadalach	*late*	**ro (& lenition)**	*too (i.e. more than is appopriate)*

Verbs

chaidh	*went*	**gun deach**	*that ... went*
an deach	*did ... go?*	**nach deach**	*that ... did not go*
cha deach	*did not go*	**rach**	*go*

Nouns

ceòl (m)	*music*	**an ceòl**	*the music*
		leis a' cheòl	*with the music*

Prepositions

dhan	*to (the)*

In addition to the two **auxiliary verbs** 'to be', there are ten irregular verbs in Gaelic. Most of these are extremely commonly used (which is why they have become irregular), and it is impossible to communicate adequately in Gaelic without a thorough knowledge of them. The irregular verbs are: ***ràdh***, ***faicinn***, ***cluinntinn***, ***dèanamh***, ***faighinn***, ***dol***, ***tighinn***, ***breith***, ***toirt***, and ***ruigsinn***. You have already encountered the verbal nouns and past tenses of ***ràdh***, ***faicinn***, ***cluinntinn***, and ***dèanamh***:

Ag ràdh - saying

An tuirt? - did ... say?

Thuirt - said

Cha tuirt - did not say

Gun tuirt - that ... said

Nach tuirt - that ... did not say

A' faicinn - seeing

Am faca? - did ... see?

Chunnaic - saw

Chan fhaca - did not see

Gum faca - that ... saw

Nach fhaca - that ... did not see

A' cluinntinn - hearing

An cuala? - did ... hear?

Chuala - heard

Cha chuala - did not hear

Gun cuala - that ... heard

Nach cuala - that ... did not hear

A' dèanamh - doing, making

Rinn - did, made

Cha d' rinn - did not do, did not make

Gun d' rinn - that ... did, that ... made

Nach d' rinn - that ... did not do, that ... did not make

These four verbs are very important and you must learn them off by heart before moving on any farther. In the next few units, you will be learning the past tenses of the other six irregular verbs. You will also learn the future tenses of all ten irregular verbs. As is the case with regular verbs, there are only three 'tenses': past, future and conditional. The conditional of both regular and irregular verbs will be introduced near the end of this course, but will be covered in more detail in the next part of the course.

Eacarsaich 21A. A' cleachdadh nan gnìomhairean a bha agad roimhe

Cuir Gàidhlig air:

1. I saw Donald when I was working in the town.
2. Did you hear that music?
3. Jean said that she was busy yesterday.
4. We made the food because we were hungry.

Past Tense of the verb 'to go'

As you know, the verb 'to go' is **dol**. The root is **rach** ('go!'), but the past tense is not related to this at all. The independent form of the past tense is **chaidh**:

Eisimpleirean:

Chaidh mi dhachaigh tràth.
I went home early.

Chaidh Iain don bhaile an-dè.
Iain went to town yesterday.

Chaidh iad sa chàr.
They went in the car.

The dependent form is **deach**:

An deach thu dhan chèilidh aig deireadh na seachdain?
Did you go to the ceilidh at the weekend?

Cha deach sinn fada, oir bha an aimsir cho dona.
We didn't go far, because the weather was so bad.

Thuirt Mairead gun deach i ann.
Margaret said that she went there.

As always, you use the independent form of the verb to answer 'yes' to a question and the negative, dependent form to answer 'no':

An deach? - did ... go?

Chaidh - yes

Cha deach - no

Eacarsaich 21B.

Cuir Gàidhlig air:

1. Did you do?
2. She did not hear.
3. We said.
4. They made.
5. Calum heard.
6. Marsaili went.
7. Did he say?
8. Iain did not go.
9. You (pl) said.
10. Did Ceit go?

Other information:

In many dialects, the root of **dol** is not **rach**. One of the most common variants is **theirig**. Some speakers mainly use **thalla** (from **falbh**) to tell people to 'go', but in Islay **thalla** means 'come'. Despite the variations in the root, the independent form of the past tense is always **chaidh**. In some dialects, an older version of the dependent form has been retained: **deachaidh**. This works in the usual way: **an deachaidh?**, **cha deachaidh**, **gun deachaidh**, **nach deachaidh**.

Another verb often used with the sense of 'go' is **gabhail**. It is especially common to use the root/imperative form when giving directions: **gabh**, 'go', 'start'.

Possessive Pronouns

You encountered the possessive pronouns or adjectives in the workbook already, but here they are again:

mo - my
do - your
a - his, its (m.)
a - her, its (f.)

ar - our

ur - your (pl)
an/am - their (**b, f, m, p** rule applies here)

The first three, ***mo***, ***do*** and ***a*** (masc.) all cause lenition of a lenitable noun:

mo charaid - my friend
do charaid - your friend
a charaid - his friend, its friend (m.)

The other four do not cause lenition:

a caraid - her friend, its friend (f.)
ar caraid - our friend
ur caraid - your (pl) friend
an caraid - their friend

> Note the similarity between 'the friend' and 'their friend' in Gaelic. The context usually helps you with this.

When the noun begins with a vowel, the possessives act as follows:

mo : m'
do : d'
a (his) : Ø

The symbol Ø is being used here to indicate that the word disappears entirely.

Eisimpleirean:

m' athair - my father
d' athair - your father
athair - his father, its father (m.)

> Note that 'his father' is exactly the same as 'father' or 'a father'. The context will usually help you work out which it is.

The feminine possessive is separated from a noun that begins with a vowel by the insertion of *h-*:

a h-athair - her father, its father (f.)

The plural first and second forms cause **eclipsis** of a noun that begins with a vowel:

ar n-athair - our father
ur n-athair - your (pl) father

The third person plural is **an** before a vowel, and can therefore look like a definite article. On the rare occasions when the context does not tell you which it is, it usually doesn't really matter.

> ### Other information:
>
> An older form of **ur** is **bhur**: some speakers still use it, and you will definitely come across it in the written language.
>
> Some people write an apostrophe before a noun that starts with a vowel to indicate that the third person masculine pronoun is being implied:
>
> 'athair - his father

There is no formal or technical difference in usage between the possessive idioms with *aig* and these possessive articles. However, in practice, speakers do use them in different situations. As a rough guide, use the possessive pronouns with things which are physically or emotionally close to you, such as clothes, family members and parts of the body. For most other things, it is possible to use either:

an càr agam - my car
mo chàr - my car

It is very important to learn these possessives and to familiarise yourself with the patterns of lenition, **eclipsis**, etc. Like the other pronouns, these ones also join up with some of the prepositions to form their own sets of prepositional pronouns. When they do, they retain their lenition and **eclipsis** patterns.

Unit 21 Reading Texts:

Chaidh mi cuairt a Leòdhas o chionn trì seachdainean. 'S e àite inntinneach a th' ann. 'S e eilean a th' ann, ach tha e ceangailte ri eilean eile: Na Hearadh! Tha agad ri dhol ann air a' bhàta no air plèan. Tha bàta mòr brèagha aca, an t-*Eilean Leòdhais*, a thog Ferguson Shipbuilders ann an Glaschu ann an 1995. Tha plèan a' dol ann cuideachd gach latha bho àiteachan mar Obar Dheathain, Inbhir Nis agus Glaschu.

Chaidh mise ann air a' bhàta. 'S e latha math, soilleir a bh' ann, agus bha sealladh math agam bhon bhàta. Chunnaic mi peileagan bhon bhàta, agus bha mi air bhioran le sin. Chan fhaca mi muc-mhara an turas seo, ach tha sin ceart gu leòr.

'S e eilean mòr a th' ann an Leòdhas. Tha mu 18,500 dhaoine a' fuireach ann. Tha Gàidhlig aig a' chuid as motha de na daoine. O chionn beagan bhliadhnachan, 's ann anns a' Ghàidhlig a bha daoine a' bruidhinn fad na h-ùine, ach a-nis tha mòran Beurla ann. Tha beathaichean inntinneach ann, mar iolairean, fèidh, agus ròin.

'S e Steòrnabhagh am baile as motha air an eilean. Chuala mi gu bheil faisg air leth de na daoine air an eilean a' fuireach ann an Steòrnabhagh. O chionn beagan bhliadhnachan, rinn mòran dhaoine am beòshlaint ag iasgach, ach chan eil sin cho cumanta an-diugh.

Is toil leam Leòdhas, agus tha mi ag iarraidh a dhol ann a-rithist aon latha.

cuairt: a trip, a journey
Leòdhas: Lewis
eilean: island
o chionn: ago
inntinneach: interesting
ceangailte: joined
Na Hearadh: Harris
tha agad ri: you have to
gach: each, every
mar: like, such as
sealladh: view
peileag(an): porpoise(s)
muc-mhara: whale
turas: a time, a trip, a journey
a' chuid as motha: the majority
fad na h-ùine: all the time
beathach, beathaichean: animal(s)
iolaire(an): eagle(s)

fiadh, fèidh: deer
ròn, ròin: seal(s)
Steòrnabhagh: Stornoway
as motha: biggest
beòshlaint: living, livelihood
ag iasgach: fishing
cumanta: common

Reminder of lenition
- The consonants which can lenite are: b, c, d, f, g, m, p, s, t
- The consonants which never lenite in writing are: l, n, r, sg, sm, sp, st

Unit 21 Dialogue:
Sorcha and Màiri take their purchases home with them

SORCHA:	Tha mi air mo dhòigh glan le mo chòta ùr!
MÀIRI:	Tha do chòta a' coimhead brèagha. Tha e a' dol glè mhath leis na brògan sin.
SORCHA:	Nach eil mo bhrògan brèagha cuideachd?
MÀIRI:	'S ann glè bhrèagha a tha iad!
SORCHA:	An toil leat dath mo bhaga? Chan eil mise cinnteach a-nis...
MÀIRI:	Is toil, ach chan eil do bhaga a' dol gu math le do bhrògan.
SORCHA:	Chan eil. Bha mi a' smaoineachadh gun robh nuair a bha sinn anns a' bhùth, ach nis agus gu bheil sinn aig an taigh, chan eil mi cinnteach.
MÀIRI:	Ach bha spòrs againn an-diugh, nach robh?
SORCHA:	O, bha! Abair latha!
MÀIRI:	Tha mise a' dol a cheannach còta ùr a-màireach.
SORCHA:	Tha mise ag iarraidh a thighinn còmhla riut!

air dòigh: happy
air dòigh glan: very happy
còta: coat

UNIT 22: DIRECT OBJECT PRONOUNS AND PAST PARTICIPLES

Technical Terms Used in this Unit

past participle The past participle is the part of the verb which can do the job of an adjective. It generally implies that an action is completed and that that has resulted in a state which it is now describing: 'the food is all <u>eaten</u>', 'the car is <u>broken</u>', 'my thumb is <u>swollen</u>'.

Faclan an Latha ... Your Daily Dose of Vocabulary

Key Words and Phrases

bidh mi gad fhaicinn	*I'll be seeing you*	**is aithne dhomh**	*I know (a person/place/how to do something)*
chan eil mi gad thuigsinn	*I don't understand you*	**chan aithne dhomh**	*I don't know*
an aithne dhut?	*do you know?(a person/place/how to do something)*	**gur aithne dhomh**	*that I know*

Adjectives
faiceallach — *careful*

Verbs
ag ionndrainn — *missing (somebody)*
ionndrainn! — *miss (somebody)!*

When a pronoun is the direct object with a verbal noun (e.g. 'finding you'), the pronoun usually comes *before* the verbal noun in Gaelic. The possessive pronoun is used instead of the normal pronoun, and it joins with the particle *ag*, as follows:

Ag + mo : gam
Ag + do : gad
Ag + a : ga
Ag + a : ga

Ag + ar : gar
Ag + ur : gur
Ag + an : gan; ag +am : gam

Other information:

The particle *ag*, which is written *a'* before a consonant, is actually the preposition *aig*. It is an 'aspect marker', which means that it tells you how complete the action of the verb is. The aspect marker *ag/a'* tells you that the verb is *in progress* (making it equivalent to the present participle in English, the '-ing' form).

Many speakers pronounce the first and second person singular possessives clearly when using these forms, so that they sound like *ga mo* and *ga do*, especially before consonants.

The first three in this group cause lenition (because they include the possessives which lenite):

Gam fhaicinn - seeing me
Gad fhaicinn - seeing you
Ga fhaicinn - seeing him, seeing it
Ga faicinn - seeing her, seeing it
Gar faicinn - seeing us
Gur faicinn - seeing you (pl)
Gam faicinn - seeing them

Notice that, when the verbal noun begins with **b**, **f**, **m** or **p**, the third person plural prepositional pronoun here is the same as the first person singular: ***gam***. However, the first person singular form causes lenition and the third person plural form does not:

Gam fhaicinn - seeing me
Gam faicinn - seeing them

Eacarsaich 22A. Cuir Beurla air:

1. Tha mi ga sgrìobhadh gu faiceallach.
2. Bha Mairead ga dhèanamh an-dè.
3. Cò tha gan cleachdadh?
4. A bheil thu ga h-iarraidh?
5. A bheil sibh gam fhaicinn?
6. Chan eil i gar coimhead.
7. An e Dòmhnall a tha gad thogail?*
8. Tha mi gad ionndrainn.

***togail** means 'lifting', 'raising' (including 'bringing up children') and also 'picking up' (including with the sense of meeting somebody to take them somewhere).

Eacarsaich 22B. Cuir Gàidhlig air (remember you will need to know the gender of nouns when translating 'it'):

1. It's a beautiful car: will you be driving it?
2. Jean was singing it yesterday.
3. We will be playing it tonight.
4. I was reading them this morning.

Past participles

Past participles are often used in Gaelic as adjectives or in predicative situations. Rarely, they can also be used to convey a perfect tense – however, be cautious with this, as it will sound odd to many speakers.

The **past participle** is built on the root of the verb. The ending is –*te*, and this is almost the only thing that is allowed to break the usual broad-to-broad-slender-to-slender rule. In a few words, the ending is –*ta*, which indicates that these words resisted breaking the rule. Most words retain the –*te* ending, regardless of whether they are broad or slender, though.

ithte
eaten

sgrìobhte
written

togte
built

lorgte
found

One of the most commonly used past participles is one that uses the *–ta* ending: ***pòsta***, 'married':

A bheil thu pòsta?
Are you married?

Another one is ***dèanta***, 'done, made', but you will also come across this as ***dèante***.

The time - 1

Over the next few units, we will go into more detail about telling the time. In general, telling the time is rather similar conceptually to English: i.e. it is based on the hours, half-past, and minutes to and minutes past the hour. To ask someone what time it is, you ask:

Dè an uair a tha e? - what time is it?

Or you might ask:

A bheil an uair agad? - do you have the time?

Unit 22 Reading:

'S e cànan Ceilteach a th' ann an Gàidhlig. 'S ann ann an Alba a tha daoine ga bruidhinn an-diugh, ach tha sgoilearan ag ràdh gur ann ann an Èirinn a bha i. Chan eil a h-uile duine gan creidsinn. Ach tha e soilleir gu bheil Gàidhlig ceangailte ri Gàidhlig na h-Èireann. Tha an dà chànan glè choltach ri chèile. Nuair a tha daoine le Gàidhlig na h-Èireann ag èisteachd ri Gàidhlig Albannach, tha iad ga tuigsinn, co-dhiù beagan. Agus, nuair a tha daoine le Gàidhlig Albannach ag èisteachd ri Gàidhlig na h-Èireann, tha iad ga tuigsinn, co-dhiù beagan. 'S e cànan Ceilteach eile a tha sa Chuimris. Ach chan eil Cuimris mòran coltach ri Gàidhlig. Nuair a tha daoine le Gàidhlig ga leughadh no ga cluinntinn, chan eil iad ga tuigsinn. Agus, nuair a tha daoine le Cuimris a' leughadh no a' cluinntinn Gàidhlig, chan eil iadsan ga tuigsinn nas motha. Tha an dà chànan ceangailte, ach chan e ceangal faisg a th' ann. Mar eisimpleir: tha am facal Cuimris 'plant' a' ciallachadh 'clann'. Gu h-eachdraidheil, 's e an aon fhacal a th' annta, ach chan eil daoine gam faicinn mar an aon fhacal an-diugh.

sgoilear(an): scholar(s)
a' creidsinn: believing
coltach ri chèile: alike
Cuimris: Welsh
nas motha: either
ceangal: connection
a' ciallachadh: meaning
gu h-eachdraidheil: historically

Unit 22 Dialogue:

Gòrdan, Niall and Calum are in a hurry again: this time, they need to get to their second class of the day, but none of them can remember where it is, and none of them have brought watches with them. Calum spots somebody walking past whom he recognises from Celtic Society

CALUM:	Gabh mo leisgeul!
DUINE:	Halò.
CALUM:	A bheil an uair agad?
DUINE:	Tha. Tha e dà uair feasgar.
CALUM:	Tiors, a dhuine.
NIALL:	Dà uair feasgar! Tha sinn fadalach a-rithist, a chàirdean!
CALUM:	Tha an clas a' tòiseachadh aig dà. Tha sinn ga chall!
GÒRDAN:	Bidh sinn ceart gu leòr. Is aithne dhomh an tidsear.

NIALL: Ciamar a tha sin gar cuideachadh?
GÒRDAN: Chan eil fhios a'm càit a bheil an clas, ach **tha** fhios a'm càit am bi an tidsear an-dràsta!

Gòrdan leads them to the pub, and they find not only the teacher, but also the rest of the class!

a' tòiseachadh: starting
a' call: losing, missing [i.e. missing a class, missing a programme, etc. – but not missing a person, which is ***ionndrainn***]
a' cuideachadh: helping

APPENDIX

Appendix – Prepositional Pronouns

1st person singular	**agam**	at me
2nd person singular	**agad**	at you
3rd person singular (masculine)	**aige**	at him, at it
3rd person singular (feminine)	**aice**	at her, at it
1st person plural	**againn**	at us
2nd person plural	**agaibh**	at you (plural or polite)
3rd person plural	**aca**	at them

1st person singular	**orm**	on me
2nd person singular	**ort**	on you
3rd person singular (masculine)	**air**	on him, on it
3rd person singular (feminine)	**oirre**	on her, on it
1st person plural	**oirnn**	on us
2nd person plural	**oirbh**	on you (plural or polite)
3rd person plural	**orra**	on them

1st person singular	**annam**	in me
2nd person singular	**annad**	in you
3rd person singular (masculine)	**ann**	in him, in it
3rd person singular (feminine)	**innte**	in her, in it
1st person plural	**annainn**	in us
2nd person plural	**annaibh**	in you (plural or polite)
3rd person plural	**annta**	in them

1st person singular	**dhomh**	to me
2nd person singular	**dhut**	to you
3rd person singular (masculine)	**dha**	to him, to it
3rd person singular (feminine)	**dhi**	to her, to it
1st person plural	**dhuinn**	to us
2nd person plural	**dhuibh**	to you (plural or polite)
3rd person plural	**dhaibh**	to them

1st person singular	**bhuam**	from me
2nd person singular	**bhuat**	from you
3rd person singular (masculine)	**bhuaithe**	from him, from it
3rd person singular (feminine)	**bhuaipe**	from her, from it
1st person plural	**bhuainn**	from us
2nd person plural	**bhuaibh**	from you (plural or polite)
3rd person plural	**bhuapa**	from them

1st person singular	**leam**	with me
2nd person singular	**leat**	with you
3rd person singular (masculine)	**leis**	with him, with it
3rd person singular (feminine)	**leatha**	with her, with it
1st person plural	**leinn**	with us
2nd person plural	**leibh**	with you (plural or polite)
3rd person plural	**leotha**	with them

1st person singular	rium	to me
2nd person singular	riut	to you
3rd person singular (masculine)	ris	to him, to it
3rd person singular (feminine)	rithe	to her, to it
1st person plural	rinn	to us
2nd person plural	ribh	to you (plural or polite)
3rd person plural	riutha	to them

1st person singular	dhìom	off/from me
2nd person singular	dhìot	off/from you
3rd person singular (masculine)	dheth	off/from him, off/from it
3rd person singular (feminine)	dhith	off/from her, off/from it
1st person plural	dhinn	off/from us
2nd person plural	dhibh	off/from you (plural or polite)
3rd person plural	dhiubh	off/from them

1st person singular	**asam**	from me
2nd person singular	**asad**	from you
3rd person singular (masculine)	**às**	from him, from it
3rd person singular (feminine)	**aiste**	from her, from it
1st person plural	**asainn**	from us
2nd person plural	**asaibh**	from you (pl)
3rd person plural	**asta**	from them

1st person singular	**fodham**	under me
2nd person singular	**fodhad**	under you
3rd person singular (masculine)	**fodha**	under him, under it
3rd person singular (feminine)	**fòipe**	under her, under it
1st person plural	**fodhainn**	under us
2nd person plural	**fodhaibh**	under you (pl)
3rd person plural	**fòpa**	under them

1st person singular	**romham**	before me
2nd person singular	**romhad**	before you
3rd person singular (masculine)	**roimhe**	before him, before it
3rd person singular (feminine)	**roimhpe**	before her, before it
1st person plural	**romhainn**	before us
2nd person plural	**romhaibh**	before you (pl)
3rd person plural	**romhpa**	before them

1st person singular	**tromham**	through me
2nd person singular	**tromhad**	through you
3rd person singular (masculine)	**troimhe**	through him, through it
3rd person singular (feminine)	**troimhpe**	through her, through it
1st person plural	**tromhainn**	through us
2nd person plural	**tromhaibh**	through you (pl)
3rd person plural	**tromhpa**	through them

1st person singular	**umam**	about me
2nd person singular	**umad**	about you
3rd person singular (masculine)	**uime**	about him, about it
3rd person singular (feminine)	**uimpe**	about her, about it
1st person plural	**umainn**	about us
2nd person plural	**umaibh**	about you (pl)
3rd person plural	**umpa**	about them

1st person singular	**thugam**	to me
2nd person singular	**thugad**	to you
3rd person singular (masculine)	**thuige**	to him, to it
3rd person singular (feminine)	**thuice**	to her, to it
1st person plural	**thugainn**	to us
2nd person plural	**thugaibh**	to you (pl)
3rd person plural	**thuca**	to them

nam (len.)	in my	**nar** (ecl.)	in our
nad (len.)	in your	**nur** (ecl.)	in your (pl)
na (len.)	in his	**nan**	in their
na (h-)	in her	**nam**	in their (b, f, m, p)

gam (len.)	at my	**gar** (ecl.)	at our
gad (len.)	at your	**gur** (ecl.)	at your (pl)
ga (len.)	at his	**gan**	at their
ga (h-)	at her	**gam**	at their (b, f, m, p)

ABOUT THE AUTHOR

Dr Moray Watson is Senior Lecturer and Head of Gaelic at the University of Aberdeen. He has been a university teacher for almost twenty years, at the Northern College, Aberdeen, the National University of Ireland, Galway, the University of the Highlands and Islands, and the University of Aberdeen. His publications include *An Introduction to Gaelic Fiction* (2011) and *The Edinburgh Companion to the Gaelic Language* (2010). His most recent book is a translation to Gaelic of *Alice's Adventures in Wonderland*, which will be published in 2012. He is currently translating *The Hobbit* to Gaelic. *Progressive Gaelic 1* is the first volume in a planned series of at least five textbooks that will guide beginners towards total fluency in Gaelic.

Made in the USA
Las Vegas, NV
08 March 2024